Blood & Honey Icons: Biosemiotics & Bioculinary

A Cookbook & Trauma Healing practice top analysis of South Slavic women war crimes and war survivors' inscribed memories; an experiential approach to food in conflict, domestic dwelling, agriculture and husbandry.

By

Danica Anderson

Biosemiotics:

Blood and Honey Icons:
The Pedagogy of South Slavic Female War and
War Crimes Survivors
Female Social Collective Practices

By

Danica Anderson

Biosemiotics: Blood and Honey Icons

©Copyright 2012, Danica Anderson. All rights reserved. ISBN:

Library of Congress Control Number: 2012922688

Olympia WA, 98516 USA

info@kolocollaboration.org

www.kolocollaboration.org

www.cookingwithbloodandhoney.com

Artists:

Connie Simpson

Erin Hilleary

Judith Shaw, http://judithshawart.com

Antonia McGuire

Videos:

Eugene Ahn, www.wigglefish.com

Design by www.ipublicidades.com

Cover Design by Bethann Carbone Branding Ovations

Table Of Contents

Short Overview 5

Introduction: Upon Broad Shoulders 17

Icons: Summary of Archetypal Movements 41

Hands and Feet Icon 42

Evoking the White Birch Tree Council Icon 46

Signs: Kolo Icon 52

Bogumile: Green Man, Thunder God 58

Storied Aprons 64

Porodin Dwelling Domovi (Home/Temple) 68

Mother Tongue: Spirituality of Relatedness and Connectivity 72

Maternal Fright: The Eye of Memory and Repression of Female Genealogies ...76

Weaver-Spinner Icon 80

Tree Spirits: Vila, or the Witch 84

Young Maiden Midday and Lady of Midnight 88

The Bear Goddess, The Madonna Goddess, and The Bird Goddess:

The Many Faces of the Goddess and Her Unifying Hidden Force 94

Broom: The Spiritual Practice and Art of Divination 98

Evolutionary Memory: Envisioning the Future through the Kolo 104

The Cloud Woman: Air, Clouds, Rain, and the Goddess Dodola 108

Letters of the Trees: Madrigals, or Singing Tree Rings	112
Whirlpools and Spirals: Bird and Fish Goddess	116
Invisibility and Transparency	122
Guardian Dogs	128
Pech (Round Beehive Stove)	132
Tree Rings	138
Bird Goddess	144
Yawning Bird Goddess	150
Bearing Witness, Transmigration, Metempsychosis, and Regeneration	156
Blood and Honey Icon Pedagogy Book Template	160
Blood and Honey Meta-Definitions: Overview	171
References	195
Endnotes	196

Short Overview

Blood and Honey Icons are the representation of past and present life experiences, directions passed down throughout the millennia that speak of what space we occupy in navigating our journeys through our own lives. Life experiences are vast and can be organized and understood through archetypal (first molded) properties.

The icons cannot give you the answers; only you have the answers. It is through icons, symbols and other figurative expressions that discovery and exploration of the self and the soma, or living body, begins. Icons are symbolic representations of an archetypal matrix that holds the cluster of symbols in a meaningful expression. Blood and Honey Icons explore how their representative symbolic expressions are related to each other and how the inter-relations shape and form the archetypal matrix.

The archetypal matrix is an outcome of my trauma work with the survivors of violence, wars, and holocausts. The archetypal matrix is a method for us to understand the Blood and Honey Icons and their interrelationships. The matrix is a space and place from which something originates and takes form; formative cells that resulted in the development of each icon. What this means is that, while there is an expression with each icon, your own symbolic representation is able to conjoin and add to that icon's universal expression. We all have experienced trauma and, as a result, are teachers and healers.

Blood and Honey Icons and biosemiotics can help us to begin the process of gauging how people feel about space and place and soak in complex modes of experience, such as sensorimotor (both the motor and sensory functions in the brain or neurological structures underlying these functions), tactile, visual, and conceptual modes of thought and action.

The linguistic element in Blood and Honey Icons is what I call biosemiotics. Our bodies and biology, such as our brain and neurological system, have a unique linguistic, or language, that is not fully translated into our twenty-six letter alphabet and words. Neuroscience tells us that the oldest part of the brain, the limbic system, is autonomic, and we are not consciously in control of its functions. Honed through millions of years of threatening and frightful episodes, the foundation of life experiences is wired into our neurological system. The wisdom of millions of years of life experiences cannot be readily realized or expressed but prefers symbolic and iconic pathways. The reality is that our autonomic language—or our brains and bodies—will certainly not fit into our limited vocabulary or alphabet.[1]

Biosemiotics bridges and communicates the gap but is flexible enough to encompass the interdisciplinary fields of archeology, archaeomythology, matriarchal studies, engendered cultural somatic psychology, neuropsychology, evolutionary biology, semiotics, and mnemonics.

Cards

The Blood and Honey Icons card deck is a hands-on experience and practice. The cards contain the same information found online and in the book. The cards are a kinetic form through which the user is able to experience the tactile process of the cards.

Arrange the selected Icons in concentric circles, called the dendrology, or nest map. Apply the pie chart with the four kolo avenues over this. (Read the kolo avenue section for meanings.)

Interpret the meaning of the kolo avenue and the Blood and Honey Icon as it pertains to your life. There are no wrong answers or interpretations; in fact, there are no answers or solutions. Life experiences are not to be solved but evolved from. Ask what the cards evoke within you and the symbolic information that they reveal. Use a sensory approach as opposed to a linear approach.

For the book form, randomly pick a page and leave the book open to the icon selected. Have the pie chart of concentric circles and dendrology/nest kolo avenues nearby. Place each selected icon on the pie chart and nest map. Reflect on the random selection of the icons and cluster the symbolic expression into your meaning and how this may pertain to you.

In using the ebook rather than the cards to perform a reading, randomly pick a page and place the pie chart of concentric circles and dendrology/nest kolo avenues on that page. Cluster the symbols and interpretations to make meaning of your own life experiences. Repeat the steps for the cards.

For Cup Readings

There is a natural law indicating that you should not read your own cups. Reading another individual's cups helps you to see yourself reflected in others, to realize that we are all connected.

Use tea leaves or African, Arabic, Eastern European, Turkish, South Slavic, or Slavic thick coffee grounds in demitasse cups for cup readings.

Observe in the cups any icons in concentric circles found in the dendrology/nest with kolo avenue one, two, three, and four (read kolo avenue and map of cups).

Imagine the pie chart mapping of the cup with the dendrology/nest of four concentric circles (read kolo avenue section and map of cups) overlaid on the kolo avenues.

Interpret the meaning of the kolo avenue and the pie chart mapping of the cup as it pertains to your life. There are no wrong answers or interpretations; in fact, there are no answers or solutions. Life experiences are not to be solved but evolved from. Ask what the symbolic information evokes within you. Focus on the sensory approach as opposed to the linear approach.

Dendrology/Nest Map (Pie Chart)

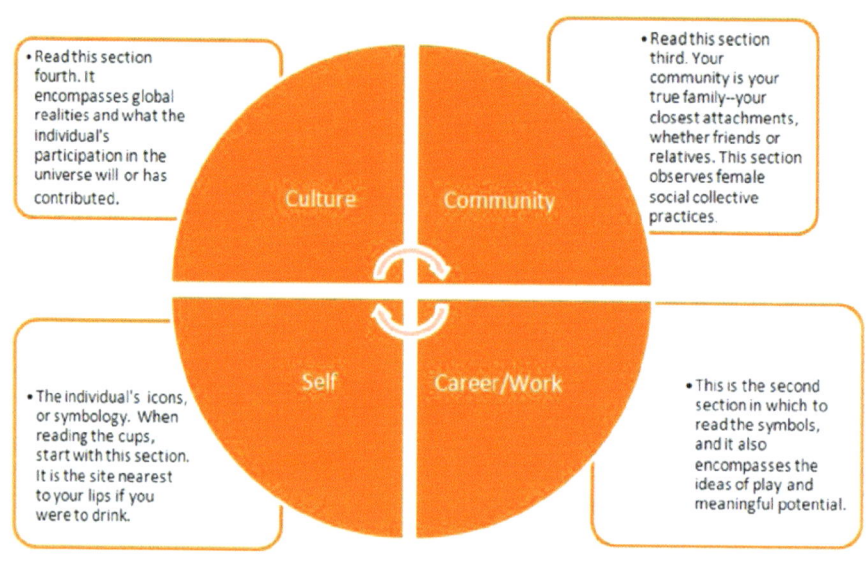

The Cup Map

Coffee Cup with the Image of a Deer

The steps you will need to follow are outlined on the website. Please visit http://www. kolocollaboration.org/ for more information. The online guide Biosemiotics: *Blood and Honey Icons* can engender an immediate response as you follow the steps outlined for the cards. Take this opportunity to journal and download your cup images or your questions about the Blood and Honey Icons you have selected. The database feature allows you to keep your own information online so that you can identify any brilliant clusters and collections of Blood and Honey Icons that express your life's experience. Journaling of the icons and cups can be partnered with a dream section where you can record your dreams to interpret their meaning. Remember that you are always the final interpreter of your dreams, cups, and Blood and Honey Icons.

The outcome of the cards, book, ebook, and web resources is learning about ourselves and life itself. We have the capacity to discern how the attitudes we are using in our interpretations help to formulate life-affirming postures and actions. Essentially, these attitudes and my kolo trauma work across the globe use trauma as an intensive learning opportunity through which we see that reality is actually where we create our life and resulting meaning.

Blood and Honey Icons Pedagogy

The art of cup readings: Biosemiotics, Mnemonics, and Female Social Collective Practices

The Balkan War in the 1990s made headlines across the globe. Each time I read or heard the word "Balkans," I felt instinctive fear and grief regarding the constant wars in the former Yugoslav regions. When I hear the term Balkans, I think of mayhem and violence. As the daughter of Serbian refugees, immigrants from WWII, I immediately engage in survival mode through a physical reaction to trauma. The genocidal and gynocidal acts perpetrated against my family occur across our planet. When such terrible violence becomes global, and thus often archetypal, an entire population can become traumatized. Instead of healthy reactions, a whole people can experience the fight or flight reaction, which leads to trauma.

How could I be so irreversibly triggered by one word; trauma? More importantly, I knew that my whole body was listening and reacting to the word Balkan and the war in former Yugoslavia, especially with all the media attention adding to the melee long before my brain was translating words. Even more impactful was my realization that my aunts, uncles, and cousins in the former Yugoslavia were in the middle of holocaustic violence yet again, as if my great-grandmother's experience of WWII, my grandmother's survival of WWII, and my mother's survival of a concentration camp was not enough. As a result of the intense emotional state of the fight/flight cycle, I had a startling insight that my body learns intensively throughout my life span.

The power of a simple word triggered myriad memories because of what it symbolized and how my body responded to hearing the word trauma spoken. This most likely originated in my childhood, as I did not speak English until I was seven, despite being in the Chicago school system. My parents struggled to learn English after they immigrated, and when I did learn to speak English, I was the interpreter for them at a very young age. One experience that caused my very physical being to recoil from hearing a single word occurred when a retail clerk spat on my mother in a dress shop in the Near North neighborhood of Chicago. My mother's posture, already the mold of a victim, now worsened significantly and visibly. The term 'DP' was unknown to me at the age of nine, and my teacher explained to me the next day that it stood for "displaced person." Because I lacked language skills to face these encounters where fear coiled into intergenerational trauma response, I learned to express myself instead through symbols and icons. As a result, I was unencumbered by words and was able to translate the world around me into archetypal symbols.

I observed that the many WWII Yugoslav refugees in our Serb community remained strangely silent about the concentration camps. My experience of the fight/ flight cycle through observing the survivors and refugees around me caused my own trauma. Although I was not born during WWII and I did not live in the former Yugoslavia during the Balkan War, it was if I were present and strangely connected to the survival mechanisms of those in my community who had experienced the horrors of that time.

I transformed the terror and trauma by accessing the rich experiential presence I found in observing my response to the word Balkan, which was in the media constantly. This was a true pedagogy, an active way to learn about the global impact of the Balkan War. My response underscores the notion that we all are predisposed toward symbolic, humanistic insights.

What if this neurological capacity to survive by forging memories and responses were used for intensified learning, not for violence, fear, and power? I knew that there had to be another use for the survival mechanism that is now subsumed and consumed in violence, wars, and relentless trauma. In my research to pinpoint a time in the past when our survival mechanisms were transformed into art forms of thriving and intensified learning environments, I found a vast pool of life experiences from the past to the present moment from which to draw.

Yet I wondered how a word could be of such great impact on me but not others. The obvious conclusion is that it is dependent on the life experiences of the individual. Life experiences are a storehouse, an archive greater than that of our meager libraries, which, though they are substantial in their own right, barely make a dent in the human mind and our responses to the environment. Science is just now beginning to explain how our genetic materials are shaped by the environment; we are connected to and formed by our surroundings rather than forming, whether physically or emotionally, in isolation. The resulting human design and our potential for experiencing are therefore highly plastic. We can mold our bodies to our environments just as our environments mold us. Herein lies the pedagogy of Blood and Honey Icons.

The Blood and Honey Icons pedagogy is a learning structure that is both iconic and symbolic. Studies on infants and children have shown that the iconic, such as body language or symbols, can be understood by the fetus, children, and adults. We are neurologically connected to the environment through our "felt" senses. Babies' crying and sudden giggles or smiles portray their "felt" states of emotions and, more critically, how intimate they are with their bodies and their environment. In fact, this knowledge is not dependent on words. Yet, as we all know, everyone around a baby immediately understands the baby's "felt" state when she makes it known.

Because I did not speak English until the second grade, I could not have understood what was happening in the Chicago school system unless there was a symbolic translation. The application of mnemonics, principles of memory, and iconic representative qualities helped me understand the world around me and translate it into terms that I could comprehend, just as a picture can express a thousand words. This is prime real estate for learning and realizing the full power of iconic or symbolic events to which our bodies and feelings respond.

What results from a simple word or term, such as my example of "Balkan," has the capacity to ignite deep feeling, fostering intensified learning environments. As a result of my own traumatic life experiences, taken into an intensified learning application, we can see features of depth where passion, awe, or curiosity are present and feeling states. Now note that our classrooms, from training to teaching environments, do not use this approach. Yet, in my kolo trauma work across the globe, our experiences and what we learn from them use healing methods, ranging from the medical to the psychological. Additionally, research on learning has shown that curiosity and awe are significant indicators of learning and neurologically important since the brain is plastic, having the capacity to imprint new information, memory, and learning no matter the age, race, or gender of the person. While students claim that they "love" math or political science, their interest is a pseudo form, or skipping over the surface with a narrow range of perspective. Instead, we should use the love of an object or subject to focus on in-depth learning with curiosity, awe, and wonder serving as guides.

Interestingly, symbolic and iconic representations, mythologies, and fables that are spoken, sung, and danced become potent places of learning and communication, speaking the same language as our bodies and brains. Memory is at the core of learning and the more *felt* the experiences, the more the memory is imprinted. We are wired neurologically to the environment and to the depth of our feelings. Students live their passions while practicing their curiosity in an open and wide range of inquiry that does not lead to answers but rather suggests meaningful journeys.

Given that our bodily senses are wired neurologically for survival, we have not explored the intricate relationships that exist in our flesh and blood to assess our environment. Perinatal research has discovered that hearing is the first sense that babies develop in the womb and the last sense to go before we die. The intricate neurology tied to feeling states is an extraordinary work of art in the technology of learning and evolving. In the complex brain, the limbic system—specifically the almond-shaped amygdala and anterior cingulate gyrus—has evolved over millions of years by responding to threat and fear with the goal of survival.[3] Located deep in the center of the brain, the walnut-sized limbic system is the place to learn invaluable skills and record life-saving memories through affective and feeling states. The result is that we have a well-honed tool for combating violence because of its powerful ability to change rapidly and translate meaning in an instant.

A prime example of an image that has changed significantly in meaning is the eighty-thousand-year-old swastika. After WWII, the swastika was stripped of its previous connection to the sun and sun worship and imbued with Hitler's message. So powerful was this association that the swastika is now universally recognized as a symbol of genocide. Few knew at the time that the WWII concentration camps included ethnic and culturally diverse peoples such as the Serbians, Roma people, and those who would not be complicit in the unnatural violence against the Jewish population.

Within the last couple of generations, the terms "Balkans" and "swastika" have, through the properties of mnemonics, developed a counter-memory that quickly erased their ancient associations. The same social memory change occurred with Aryan groups, gangs utilizing the swastika to perpetuate their hatred of various groups, love of violence, and worship of what the Nazis accomplished.

A symbol that was once worshipped as the Goddess (female icon) in the Paleolithic and Neolithic eras now sees the female chained to second class citizenry, a socio-economic impact that has her and her children in poverty or barely subsisting on low wages. In fact, Julie Mertus's humanitarian research after the Balkan War revealed that eighty percent of worldwide refugees are women and children.[4]

Observing the power of the counter-memory to eradicate thousands of years of meaning based on our ancestors' life experiences also suggests an intimate look at intensified learning capacities that trigger memory—the true symbolic representation—in our genes. We cannot overlook the fact that, during pregnancy and the first year of life, the mother is integral in the child's development. Neurological studies show that our brain development, both in the womb and during the first year of life, depends on the mother.[5] The mother's input, both physical and emotional, is critical to the development of the child during the period of his greatest neurological development, which is gestation and the first year of life. We stand in awe of this process, in which the mother is integral and the extraordinary pace of learning and development occurs with no words. If we understand this implication, we can see how important it is for programs and policies in humanitarian aid agencies to focus on this critical aspect. Furthermore, the secondary status of women and children globally, along with poverty levels, provides a chilling insight on violence and its impacts on the most vulnerable.

This finding also indicates that we cannot escape the impact of the mother's trauma during pregnancy and throughout her children's early years. Considering Mertus' statistic of the number of female refugees globally, we can understand just how the intergenerational transmission of fear, flight, fight, and genocidal or gynocidal memories is perpetuated. If we look at it another way, the classroom for learning intensives is the womb, and the child's affective-feeling states are based on the mother's life experiences.

Finally, modern science is acknowledging the female's critical role in fostering intensified learning environments from the womb throughout her and her children's life spans. Biosemiotics and mnemonics are our mother's intangible heritage, difficult to describe yet so immediately perceived and understood. Many dismiss the mother's cooing talk to her infant and the myriad ways to communicate with children in pre-verbal stages as nonsense.

Through her daily life, her domestic arts and raising children, we come face to face with an exquisite and elegant intensive learning classroom and learning tools that are beyond our twenty-six-letter alphabet.

We can explore how mothers and child-rearing manifest culture, originating language so as to allow social memory. Female social collectives are, in themselves, acts of remembering that are continuously layered with each generation's life experiences. This architectural pedagogical structure for intensified learning begins with the mother and child bonding and being emotionally moved together.

We need to look at what really happens when we are exposed to catastrophic violence or subtle forms of hostility that devalue the female gender. We are shown again and again that women are targeted in violence, removing the time-honored meaning from the mother's original context and culturally specific her/ historical perspectives, specifically her role in rearing children and motherhood. Violence, since it is fear-based, instantly overrules the love for our mothers and/ or anything remotely feminine; in particular, violence erases our ancestors' life experiences. Violence is a catastrophic form of trauma which our brains record; it becomes intergenerational because we are neurologically wired to learn any form of survivorship skills. With violence and fear, love cannot exist. These memories that shaped our species are essential to our continued growth.

This overriding of the true value and depth of intensified learning that the mother and child bond provides on a biological level speaks to the core of learning. Dependent on memory, intensified learning within parameters of awe or curiosity is the most integral feature in our neurological system and the most impacted when we are frightened into relying on our survival instincts.[6] Stand back and think about your reaction to stress or a traumatic event; in these instances, memory is often fragmented. A mother who is with her child when she faces stress and trauma experiences significant memory impact. The need to survive erases the energy the mother needs to foster an intensified learning environment for her child. When you reflect on significant memorable events in your life that were "the happiest times" or even hilarious incidents, those memories do not fade but instead empower us toward a more meaningful existence.

Memory is a result of learning with intense and rapid neurological development that starts in the womb. Throughout life, this capacity to learn appears through mostly negative and trauma-filled experiences, not those of curiosity, awe, wonder, kindness, high regard, or unconditional love. We are sensitive and psycho-biologically attuned to symbolic materials, and we are vulnerable to damaging and violent symbols. Our modern societies have normalized violence by referring to it instead as culture. I often ask during my kolo trauma work in the field how we can determine whether something constitutes culture or violence. So many things are construed as culture when they are not. Take, for example, the women's suffrage movement of the 1920s. American culture was entrenched in the notion that women did not need to be able to vote because their role was to be taken care of, a passive role. Or consider why jokes, swear words, and even songs continually heap offense on the mother or the female, but culture never seems to take this as a serious insult.

Blood and Honey Icons pedagogy purposefully experiences firsthand the exotic, true, and most ancient inner life that manifested culture in the far past, but remains elusive in our modern lives. Through icons, signs, and symbolic representations, we are encouraged to move intimately in our environments and social connections. We remember through biosemiotics, semiotics, and mnemonics the foundation of our female social collective practices, add to our extensive memory archives, and re-imagine memory as a compelling learning force.

Danica Anderson

INTRODUCTION:

Upon Broad Shoulders

"Blood and Honey" is the direct translation of the word "Balkans." The term "blood and honey" conveys the ability of Slavic languages to record past generations' life experiences and events succinctly and iconically. Blood and Honey Icon pedagogy represents and explains the experiences that make up our memories and help us translate social relations through the lens of our ancestral knowledge.

The past events in the Balkans, in particular the former Yugoslavia, have resulted in recurring catastrophic trauma. The catastrophic wars in this region have come to represent the "blood" in the term "blood and honey." Blood once was immediately understood to symbolize women's mysteries, such as menstruation, during which a woman bleeds at length without dying, and breastfeeding, when she turns blood into sweet milk—"honey"—to nourish her child. In fact, childbirth itself is a female mystery of blood.

Since March of 1999, I have been in Bosnia-Herzegovina, shoulder to shoulder with women who are war and war crimes survivors. The best sessions and bonding memories—"honey"—with the survivors involved cup readings. In the aftermath of war, the meals they made and the invitations for tea and coffee heightened their warm female social collective practices. When they had nothing, they realized they had everything.

My own childhood as the daughter of immigrant refugees from the former Yugoslavia is a lived example of the never-ending nature of war. From the 1950s to the 1980s, no child abuse laws or domestic violence laws existed in the United States; in fact, rape did not become a war crime until the late 1990s. This was well after the Balkan War and the conflicts in Asia and Africa had resulted in countless rapes and other abuses. To represent such crimes is a monumental task that acknowledges the profound incapacities of a twenty-six letter alphabet to convey the true impact of these traumas and highlights the exclusion of females in its deliberations. How does a law fully represent and symbolize abuse and rape?

Blood and Honey Icons pedagogy consists of chains of memories, "happenings" in images highlighting the meaningful moments of our narratives. With our memories, we can fully represent in all forms—not just words—the material repository for what is intangible and definitely illegible in a twenty-six letter alphabet.

The impact of the never-ending war that figures so predominantly in my childhood appears in a family member's narrative of my mother's survival in a concentration camp. My mother never talked about it or mentioned her past or her mother, my grandmother. My mother found power in forgetting because of the shame that invaded her capacity to articulate the gynocide—the mass murder of anything feminine—that she witnessed. Perhaps survivors realize that, long after the violence and abuse, the rule of law and courts re-traumatized the victims of the wars they survived despite their intention to seek justice.

Curiously, my mother's Slavic culinary art and her joy in dancing the South Slavic round dances—kolos—were in part her only empowered defenses, iconic features against the holocaustic events in her life. I realized that I entered a domain in which traditionally feminine practices such as cooking and dancing facilitated the ultimate circle of reciprocity poised upon the act of learning and memories.

The intergenerational nature of trauma is apparent to me as it is to Bosnian women, some of whom survived two wars in one century. The repetition of the intergenerational trauma is most likely because of their indigenous female social collective practices and the mother-child bond that perpetuates instructional approaches for a meaningful life is erased with victimhood. The folk round dances (kolos) are an example of this handing down of female social collective practices through the generations. My own parents, immigrants with only an elementary school education, taught us to repeat the dance steps. Moving through the kolo dance steps within the circle is a method of healing trauma for South Slavs. The kolo is, in essence, a trauma response that calms and soothes. As we perform repetitive actions of a somatic nature (known as a sensorimotor psychotherapy), having our bodies in a circle structure that does not repeat—but perhaps cancels out or fights against—violence and trauma events is an age-old healing practice.

The culinary arts my mother and other mothers performed in their North Side Chicago neighborhoods are actually what I term "bioculinary" female social collective practices. South Slavic women knew to brew the proper chai (tea) for colds, diabetes, and high blood pressure. The female social collective indigenously understood which foods to eat seasonally—actually the appropriate time when food is best foraged or harvested. My father would meet the train carrying the grapes from California and make homemade wine, which each Fall we would press from the grapes in the basement. Their South Slavic relations with the Earth could not be severed in their new country, even in the midst of a busy city. They transmitted these practices to me; I remember stomping the grapes for the homemade wine in a wooden barrel in our dark, humid basement.

The refugees and immigrants in my parents' community banded together, preserving female social collectives within their religious affiliations, which were built upon memories and lost locales. However, religious doctrines are caustic to females in a variety of edicts and doctrines. The female social collective thrived despite organized religion's denigration of the female and her roles. Social memory, particularly in South Slavic practices, has evocative soma integration, or the inclusion of the body. Many of the original associations and meanings may have been lost over time because of the continual devaluing of female status and gender. However, what I have observed in my childhood and through holocaust survivors is that the female social collective has implicit continuity and is resurrected by the women's life experiences. Essentially, the experiences of the survivors' mothers and grandmothers are present in the female social collective memories and practices. A good example is the medical fact-gathering that I do in the field;

for example, I have repeatedly discovered that mothers and daughters usually become menopausal at the same point in each of their lives. Many women in the former Yugoslavia also used herbs to help them heal and simply survive during and after the Balkan War, which mirrored the practices of their mothers and grandmothers in WWI and WWII.

The Serbian Orthodox church includes their female social collective community based on the Mesolithic kolo. An example is the women's association, often named for the circle of sisters, or *kolo sestara* (sisters or sorority) responsible for the catering, choirs, fundraising, and Sunday school for the church. The kolo dances, songs, and feasts celebrating the holy holidays help to preserve ancestral memories. The icons hanging on the altar are reconstructed and integrated, and their specific images and symbols provide a place for memory to exist.[7] However, women are not allowed behind the altar or to take communion if they are menstruating or have recently given birth. Their life-giving practices magnify the endless uroboric circle in which the beginning is the end and the end is the beginning.

The uroboric intergenerational transmission of female social collective practices facilitates mindfulness and allows the gathering of women in a circle-kolo within patriarchal religious institutions. Without the patriarchal structures of worship to control women, women's circles would have raised fear in men. During the Middle Ages, the Catholic Inquisition committed the world's worst holocaust against females, killing millions for over three hundred years and sealing an innate fear within females of gathering in solidarity or in circles unless strictly sanctioned by male-dominated institutions and family units.

Yet the Slavic references to Mother Church and Mother Land realize the transformation and the capacity to instill the intergenerational memories that once honored the Earth as the Great Mother of Life. Those memories, operating under the radar and underground, maintain their exquisite and strictly Pagan associations that signal the presence of female social collectives thriving—not just surviving— despite the violence toward her sex.

Female social collectives act as receptacles of ancestral memories and as mnemonics, reactivating the ascendancy of symbols intertwined with narratives. Their domestic instruments, from demitasse cups to the coffee pot with its smaller neck at the top (called *Jesva* in Serbo-Croatian), allow the same context of memory and imagery; their mere shapes constitute the material repository that brews up memory-mnemonics. The *Jesva*, a universal image, is found throughout the Balkans and in Russia, the Middle East, Iran, and Sudan. Many times while I was in Sudan, Turkey, or in other Muslim countries, women would mention a kinship with the Bosnian coffee pot as being universal in their lives and culture, often speaking of how they or their mothers made the coffee—and, of course, theirs is the best. I encountered the practical application of an ancient visual icon in a mere coffee pot, the *Jesva*. Like the coffee shops in North America, Sudanese women-only salons allowed women to brew up coffee and circle around each other to share their experiences, despite the caustic restrictions in place on their gender.

In the former Yugoslavia, Bosnia-Herzegovina, or at the Serb Hall in Chicago, Saturday night dances, called *Sevdah* or *Sevdalinka*, demonstrate the entire environment of South Slavic female collective practices from the bioculinary to the lively and rhythmic kolos danced by young and old, shoulder to shoulder. These dances fit into the traditional genre of former Yugoslav folk music and kolo dances. South Slavic Bosnians celebrate Ramadan with the kolo and feasts. The Catholic holiday called the Day of Bread in Bosnia-Herzegovina is another religious holiday with Paleolithic and Pagan associations that suggests a considerable overlap of memories. As you can see, iconic representations are universal among religions and ethnic groups, but the same inner guidance and validation can only appear if their origins are millennia old. Our ancestors' memories are repeated in current generations. In other words, when I dance the kolo and its algorithmic dance steps, I know my Mesolithic ancestors have danced the steps and that their life experiences are stamped into modern generations.

Little did I realize that my love of and joy in the kolos and my ability to read the cups came from the intensified learning my mother provided, or how it would play such a significant part in my life and the lives of those suffering from violent trauma. I can say that the cups and the kolo sent me across the globe to Bosnia-Herzegovina, Sri Lanka, India, Africa, and to Haiti nine days after the earthquake. Sensing the indigenous female social collective in my life as an ancient science instead of accepting the current global view of women's work as valueless, I went on to be the first in my family to have a college education—a master's degree in psychology— and to be working on my doctorate in Somatic Psychology. Learning from my global experiences and observing the origins of science itself in the indigenous female social collective prompted my path to higher education. I realized through my lived experiences that the female social collective needed to be represented in the sciences, not excluded. Somatic Psychology allows the living body to be included in its science and functions as a universal learning application.

My curriculum was not just academic; I found it in the informal classroom that read cups and dreams, acknowledging synchronicity through iconic language with my friends and colleagues who gathered at the table to participate in ancient social collective practices, nourished by meals that my own hands had created in the tradition of my female ancestors.

I am indebted to these women and their families; they are the real, natural, environmental scientists whose way of living provided me with instruction in and understanding of biosemiotics through a trauma treatment and training that heals their families and local communities. What I learned was self-sustainability in daily life and practices that can be performed in any given moment. Upon their broad shoulders, the Slavs (including Russian Slavs and South Slavs) help us to recognize that trauma is an intensified learning process, a classroom to transform obstacles into opportunities of curiosity, awe, and wonder, as opposed to a mental disorder.

Engagement in Reading the Cards and The Cups

Writing the material for this book prompted me to consider what the body-mind circular process is and its iconic, rather than verbal, nature. I understood that it could not possibly be conveyed on the page or the Internet. Additionally, the feminine foundation of the material, the devaluing of women's work and domestic arts, and her second-class citizenry are severe obstacles to presenting the origins of science as being her work and life experiences. A good example of this predicament is shown with the study of the Mayan language, Tzeltal. Scientists simply could not understand why the language of the descendants of the Mayans had no separate words for the right or left arm or leg.[8]

Certainly, the researchers could judge the omission of right or left arm/leg as coming from a primitive culture. But is this accurate? Ken Wilbur's quantum psychology studies report that "dualistic and symbolic knowledge is at once the brilliance and the blind-spot of science and philosophy, for it allows a highly sophisticated and analytical picture of the world itself, but however illuminating and detailed these pictures may be, they remain just that—pictures."[9] Wilbur points out that when analysis or codification of the material occurs, it is replaced by symbolism.[10] Female social collective practices, their intangible heritage, are a lived way of understanding beyond symbolic representations. We can identify how symbols mirror one's processes and how the female social collective has been practicing Wilbur's quantum psychology for millennia. Studies of cave art and script reveals that signs on archaeological artifacts from the Mesolithic and Upper Paleolithic are certainly the inspiration, if not clarification into icons and symbols, for our ancestors' life experience to be evoked into present day.

We do know that, across the globe, the right side of the body is privileged. According to Yi-Fu Taun's book *The Perspective of Experience,* the right arm, hand, and leg are an ideogram for what is legitimate, while the left is the profane, impure, and maleficent.[11] In fact, the meaning of sinister comes from the Latin word indicating the left side. In catastrophic situations, females are targeted as impure, and in medical science, the right side of the brain is known as female. Taun states that humans and other animals have an innate "endowment" within our sensory organs, but the difference in humans is our capacity for symbolization.[12]

If you note how icons and symbols create another space for a universal language, we can see how symbols do, in fact, manifest space and place for our life experiences. In our human geography, space and place address life experiences and our relationship to change and learning. In Taun's human geography research and ethological studies, he describe place as incurring *felt* value, while space is a sense of territory. It is the space and place of the symbolism found therein that identifies culture. In other words, we apply meaning with our felt value of life experiences. With felt values, we are compelled to assign an iconic representation or symbology to memory. While Taun admits that culture is inescapable, he acknowledges that studying the relations between space and place gives meaning to experience. Meaning, a felt value, is then merged into place. Icons, symbols, and ideograms are tools to express the nature of experience and the perspective that is the result of that study.

In fact, the missing orientation for Tzeltal's left and right is the sacred space where we exist relative to the environment and can observe it from a bird's eye view. The left side of the table, where our hand is placed during eating, is highly significant since it is a mirror of our bodies and spirits in respect to the environment we are in at the moment. The proprioceptive (sensing deep internal movements) consciousness that occurs with this orientation of the body in the environment provides a quiet awareness through which to observe your natural being. Now imagine this when dancing the kolo, shoulder to shoulder with others, or holding a cup. It is a social agreement, a South Slavic cultural moment, to deepen and gradually comprehend what is behind the symbols and scripts. All of it prompts reflection.

Past life experiences, from our ancestors to the present moment and into future generations, are lived through daily life practices. Biosemiotics are not just pictures or symbols but a mother tongue, codes of communication within female social practices and lived soma/body/brain experiences, recorded like notes on a sheet of music.

The Blood and Honey Icons, whether in card form, in cup readings, or on the web, will provide more inquiry than solutions to your questions. The end result is a learning environment or classroom, not a step-by-step self-help book with volumes of conclusions and solutions. Engagement in reading the Blood and Honey icons pedagogy and cup readings is experiential. Flow through the materials rather than searching for the quick sheet of instructions.

Biosemiotics

Intriguing new fields from computational semiotics to lexical literary semiotics reveal what the ancient practices from the *I Ching* to the tea and coffee cup readings and dream analysis have been applying for thousands of generations: the importance of context, not text, and symbolic expression. Even Carl Jung could not help but study the *I Ching* due to its semiotics and symbology. Russian Slav Mikhail Bakhtin, in the early nineteenth century and throughout Stalin's rule, developed the philosophy of language, a dialogic imagination process that is little known in the Western world. Bakhtin is a noted Semiotician who carved out concepts of heteroglossia (context over text), polyglossia (coexistence of multiple languages in the same area), and chronotope (time and space) that govern all narrative and linguistic expressions.

Although Blood and Honey Icons are an expressed female humanities specific to the Balkans, they are indigenous to all. Icons are ideographs and ideograms symbolizing the full scope of movement and meaning in one glance. Blood and Honey Icons are a focused lens onto the South Slavic females that we can find across the globe and in our own lives. Organizing the material is about having a circular flow of information, however, not the expected linear structure that science demands.

What are Blood and Honey Icons?

Somatic (living body) pedagogical and instructional arrangements with images of Paleolithic and Neolithic artifacts or archeological remnants describe embodied movements. Archetypal somatic patterns are best read through signs, symbols, icons, and the body. The Blood and Honey Icons are memories that significantly shaped South Slavic-Slavic communal memory and can most likely be found within your own life experiences. Adding your expression to a collective pool of archetypes, icons, and symbolic expression provides a "felt sense" of how we are all connected.

Icons are images, paintings, and signs. Memnonia, the fusing of memory, and the phenomenology of a female domestic space and life experiences, are a co-penetrating series of memories about how people lived, recalling both events and people. Funneled into archeomythologies and archeological artifacts, the archetypes or patterns can be interpreted interchangeably to create meaningfulness, which manifests a social communal collective. Semiosis, meaning signs, symbols, and icons, and biosemiosis, meaning life, signs, symbols, and icons, refer to the act of creating signs. The difference between semiosis and biosemiosis is the presence of biology, or life essence. Icons, symbols, and signs are a script of "somatically felt" life experiences that brings immediate awareness, insight, or knowledge without words or contemporary alphabetic writing. A mnemonic, a tool using the cup readings or icons to find the archetypal patterns found in the cups or the icons that trigger "memory" and "immediate knowing," can be a formula, dance, chant, or poetic rhyme used as an aid in remembering.

More about Biosemiotics and Mnemonics

Biosemiotics, Greek for "life" and *semeion* for "sign," is a growing research field for the interpretation of biological signs and for Somatic Psychology. These sciences examine areas of proto-language or pre-verbal language accompanying the development of the brain as a study of the intricate flow of information and how it is communicated. We are all born with language, the linguistic capacity found in icons, signs, and symbols. In fact, our brains and bodies communicate and translate expressions in this iconic, representative nature. Biosemiotics challenges the theoretical portion of the sciences for their normative perspectives often exclusive of the soma/body or often with an ownership of the female soma.

Hundreds of thousands of concepts, thoughts, and perhaps radical examples of language are found in biosemiotics, semiotics, and mnemonics, which provide unique analysis of dreams and various icons, signs, and events that cross our paths. With the unlimited number of concepts and their iconic expressions, archeologists and anthropologists are able to study the linguistic origins of the various psychological fields in which we encounter symbolic and iconic references and messages to decipher and interpret.

What most do not realize is that biosemiotics and mnemonics are found in ancient cultures and shamanic traditions. The Slavs include not just Russians but South Slavic peoples (from the former Yugoslavia) who have carried the salient biosemiotic dimensions through their social collective practices founded in somatic (living body/brain) and neurobiological processes. The efficacy of Slavic thaumaturgy (miracle-making) is but the miracle of our bodies, the neurological network and our brains plugged into our environment and life experiences. It is a language, a code, much like our digital technology; we are plasma computers with affective states for guidance and a storehouse of memories cataloged in our DNA. Our bodies hold the memories of not just our life experiences but those of our ancestors.

Our bodies' symbolic codes are littered throughout Slavic references to "Moist Mother Earth"[13] and the Slavic Baba Yaga, Mother Nature incarnate archeomythologies. Slavic people refer to their rivers as "little mothers," and in this and other ways, Slavic myths present us with embedded female humanities and culture practices. This makes sense since we are all born of a woman. Just think of the archeomythologies and universal mythologies such as the fables that we read to little children. Mythologies are first person narratives saturated in rich biosemiotics, allowing for an autonomic memory throughout the generations. These fables are based on our neurological mirror neurons—learning by observing or imitating— pointing to the powerful learning environments of the gestating female and her child-rearing practices.

Storytelling is both a powerful and empowering learning environment and has evolved from archeomythologies. Stories are readily absorbed by little children and adults since they correspond to and communicate with the enormously complex neurological system, brain, and soma-body language. Science is just catching up to the fact that healing trauma means acquiring a vocabulary for events that occurred in the lives of our ancestors, the impacts of which are passed down somatically, linguistically, and genetically to the present generation. The brain's fright/flight response is at peak attention to record the skills needed in case of a future event similar to the one that caused the trauma. Many traumatized people are triggered by smells, sounds, and sights that may mirror those experienced during the traumatic event.[14] The triggers are bodily senses that are translated in iconic and symbolic communications for our neurological systems.

Biosemiotics and How the Environment Shapes our Life Experiences

Observing Mother Nature for the Slavs is a course in the wonders of the world. Preserving and maintaining what was observed and lived by ancestors, Slavic people constructed a guardianship or a living library via their biosemiotic and mnemonic approaches. The living library, our bodies, is apparent in folk traditions, female social collectives such as the round dances, embroidery, costumes, and homes. In fact, what is termed mundane or ordinary is the extraordinary capacity to understand soma language, or the "mother tongue," which again demonstrates the importance of "women's work" despite its rejection by patriarchal accounts.

Central to the sacred South Slavic archeomythologies is the mother and child bond. Only relatively recently has science caught up with indigenous female practices that acknowledged thousands of years ago how prominently the mother figures in a child's development, especially neurologically. Neuroscientist Allan Schore's research determined that the mother and child attachment is a universal biopsychosocial process, a mix of biological and somatic factors with social/cultural influences stemming from both internalized and situational processes.[15] We can say that our mother's life experiences and her actions affect her gestation and her child-rearing and that these influences manifest culture along with our language as a result. Essentially, these South Slavic female social collective experiences are imbued with somatic neuropsychological practices often conveyed in biosemiotics and mnemonic forms.

Mnemonic forms are easily observable in the Serbo-Croatian folk circle dance known as the kolo. The name kolo comes from the Slavic word for wheel and is of Indo-European origin. This suggests the migratory routes of the Slavs across and around vast geographic planes. The Serbo-Croatian word *sestara* refers to a female sorority, indicating prehistoric South Slavic female solidarity within social collectives now subsumed in Orthodox Church practices, such as a women's group doing the labors of the kitchen and Sunday School.

The algorithmic essence of the soma-geometric features found in the kolo's following of the sun and moon allowed the organization of and categories for seasons. The lunar implications were tied to the female menstrual cycles and gestational periods. The origins of the kolo, specifically the beehive ovens central to Slavic culture and their guardianship through the generations in the kolo, date from the Danube Valley and Central Europe in 29,000 BCE.[16] However, lunar calendars are found at 50,000 BCE, indicating refinement since Neanderthals engraved the symbols for the kolo and cosmos on rocks 300,000 years ago. Both the seasons and lunar cycles gave way to the calendar and to beehive ovens. The beehive oven symbolizes the sun and solar energy as well as female lunar cycles.

Russian Archeologist Boris Illich Marshak outlined the hearth mistress, who was the keeper of the fires, fireplaces, and ovens in Slavic mythologies. The hearth mistress, according to Marshak, is not a Goddess. Rather, he theorized that the hearth mistress is a female storyteller positioned at the round *pech* (oven). Therefore, the hearth mistress was the keeper of moon changes and menstrual cycles, especially related to pregnancy, and metaphorically refers to the womb as the *pech*.[17] With the round-bellied ovens and fireplaces still present in former Yugoslav regions, we can identify how Marshak was able to surmise the daily activities occurring around the hearth as a circular space and place for storytelling, including observations of lunar phases that coincided with menstrual cycles. Women's menstrual cycles and pregnancy cycles were shared as wisdom and knowledge in this intimate circle/kolo. In Slavic mythologies, pregnancy is the ultimate metaphor and mnemonic for the 360 degree circle.

Dance and music partner in the megalithic kolo, their ancient rhythms reproducing the heartbeat of the earth.[18] Biosemiotic and mnemonic features are in their songs, chants, or ten-syllable *deseterics,* poetic lines within *Zena pesme,* or women's songs.[19] Interwoven into the South Slavic music and its musical scale, attuned to the sound of the Earth turning,[20] is the evocative, solitary female voice breaking out in song, a *deseteric* ballad, whether spoken or sung. Singing in the fields as the women work helps them maintain their remarkably intimate relationship with time as they focus on the events of the present, not the events that may be prescribed in an external chronological framework. They focus on what this time is for, not what time it is.

Their tending to the hearth and family resulted in pure bioculinary practices developed by life experiences. Foraging and growing gardens to sustain themselves and their families, accompanied by medicinal herbs and lore, served as an invaluable component in female social collectives. The kolo dances depict harvesting traditions from threshing the grain to romantic relationships. Mindfully taking breaks from their labors most likely included cup readings, whether from tea or coffee. This was to synchronize a rhythm in their daily lives for somatic rest, reflection, and mindfulness.

We can see this still occurring in modern-day coffee houses. The female social collective practices and biosemiotics in Bosnia-Herzegovina are easy to observe in the prevalent cafés, or *cafanas*. Patrons drink their thick coffee in demitasse cups throughout the day and evening. Instead of reading a newspaper, many read their cups within the evocative *cafana* setting; here, they practice epigraphy (the study and deciphering of ancient inscriptions). Their study of messages and icons is the poetic canon, or what I call the Poetic College. The Poetic College turns the mundane into archeomythological study, exacting meaningfulness from the quotidian. What transpires is the continuity of female social collective practice, an eloquent, instructive, intimacy-bearing method for images and memory.

That seemingly insignificant cup readings are often devalued as nonsense or fortune-telling in fact fosters the reconstruction of memories, especially for Balkan war survivors. Remembering in the present moment for the South Slavic survivors, among others, and in a communal fashion is an act of healing and has an important feature of layering past memories. Memories found in the Blood and Honey Icons are agents in that memory is a conduit between our life experiences and those of our ancestors.

Semiotics: Tracing Ancient origins

Archeological artifacts from the former Yugoslav region revealed thousands of "scripts," or symbols, etched on the Bird Goddess figurines. According to Marija Gimbutas, a classically trained archeologist who excavated many of the Balkan Neolithic "Old Europe" sites, the region is the cradle of the spiral, a biosemiotic and mnemonic script.[21] The script appeared to conjoin archaeologies of memory, meaning that the memories of the past and ancestors are found on the Bird Goddess artifacts and other Old Europe relics, even spirals etched in the tea leaves or thick coffee grounds as representations of social memory in modern day *cafanas* or home settings. In fact, Gimbutas points to the Bird Goddess as the origin of Baba Yaga, who corresponds to Mother Nature and is now what we refer in the modern age as angels or the witch. Both angels and witches contain the symbolic element of birds, including flying abilities and migratory behaviors.

We can say that the observances of nature were catalogued in the script-icons, signs, and symbols left in the archeological remnants. The wingless zoomorphic Bird Goddess archeological figurines littering the former Yugoslav region are iconic of how birds migrate, flying in solidarity in the vast skies, often in a *V* shape which, according to Gimbutas, represents the female in archeological artifacts. Additionally, birds' nests in the trees in Slavic archeomythologies are referred to as ancestors and are seen as representing the marrying of the skies to the Earth through the tree branches and roots. After thousands of generations reading the script, a cornucopia of icons and symbols, at the bottom of the cups or in the morning sky searching for rain, the South Slavic women banked a social memory that can be continuously examined. Since our bodies retain memories in our DNA, what is taken in by the body, such as drinking the tea or coffee, naturally reappears in icons and symbols, which are the "script" of the cup reading.

Semiotics is the study and analysis of signs and symbols, including icons. The semiotic process is where the sign's meaning—its properties of analogy, likeness, and metaphor—underlines its significance. The resulting communication in the soma/body and brain language applies meaning to many interdisciplinary fields: archeology, anthropology, evolutionary biology, Jungian dream analysis, art, sandtray therapy, and somatic psychological approaches. Even more substantial is the known value of the semiotic as having important natural scientific and anthropological features, since semiotics studies cultural trends that are known to be forms of communication and language.

Memes, according to evolutionary biologists Chris Knight and Richard Dawkins, are the origins of culture. Memes are not genes or genetic material but a "portion of cultural traditions—say, a tune, an idea, or catch-phrase—which survives in the memories of successive generations of humans and is capable of evolution at a very rapid pace."[22] The lullaby a mother sings to her child, the childhood games that identify a specific culture, and both culinary and agricultural practices from recipes to timetables for planting crops are invaluable to the transmission of life. Note the shared repetitive nature of memes and female social collective practices, an intangible heritage that manifests culture as we know it.

Most important is the real intention for engagement with icons and symbols and to study the intrinsic and immanent (internal) communication purposes. In a way, our top forty music hits are very successful memes that will live across generations. We have only to think about the Beatles or even Beethoven's music, which has lived on through the centuries, to glimpse the definition of memes and how memes are repeated throughout generations. We can say, in modern terminology, that it has gone viral. The same process holds for South Slavic peoples, the kolo and a host of daily life practices repeated continuously ensure the perpetuation of memes. What better space for memes to be repeated than a table laden with food, the kolo circle, and the bottom of a cup filled with leaves or coffee grounds?

Cup Readings, Depth Work, and Archaeologies of Memory in Cups

The coffee and tea cup readings are a collaboration of the natural world between the natural order and your life. We are participants in the construction of memory in which we serve the needs and interests of our present lives. Whether we like it or not, we are immersed in and touched by the past that is everywhere.

We are moved by archeological sites or natural monuments carved from the natural elements by peoples practicing the art of memory. The archeological artifacts and monuments have an ancestral presence, displaying their salient memory images recorded in a material repository. The ancestral imagery is a mnemonic practice, the main feature of which is the continued presence of the so-called past.[23]

The same memory process happens when brewing thick coffee grounds or loose tea. In fact, the commemorative application reactivates symbols and scripts once invisible to us but that become transparent in tea leaves or grounds. It is through symbols and the script's employment of various combinations that this practice provides an entirely different genre of writing, reflecting our biological and neurological processes.

The symbols in the cup comprise an ancient text, oral traditions etched by the creation of biosemiotic script into what Slavs point to as icons. Our bodies and neurological systems communicate through illnesses, aches, pains, and also our growth pattern throughout childhood, from our sedentary postures to the graying of our hair. Symbols are a representational media possessing commemorative functions that help us to depict our mythic events.

The depth work of engaging the symbols and what they may mean to you contributes to the construction of memory for your life. The experiential nature of the cups is simply to retrieve a social memory that many Slavs practice to keep in touch with the past and our ancestors. For that matter, many historians, archeologists, and anthropologists also dig for the culturally specific contextual meanings found in symbols.

Accessing Deep Wisdom: the Phenomenological Approach

Cup readings are the earliest forms of psychological study focused on symbols. We note the many cup marks on Paleolithic and Neolithic stones, with the oldest cup marks at an estimated 80,000 years old. Carl Jung studied the Chinese *I Ching* at great length, during which he accessed and evoked the deep wisdom of the unconscious by expressing the archetypal situation relevant to any question that may be prompted by a reading in the cups or other methods.

Every ancient civilization has a method for reading the past and symbols. For the Slavs and many Middle-Eastern peoples, it is cup readings. The Mayan calendar and symbols are implicated in the construction of memory. The Tarot, the *I Ching*, Feng Shui, and cup readings are in essence a brilliant psychological tool for self- development and also have a science harmonized into their practices. Quantum physics, epigenetics, and archaeology all appear more clearly through the study of these ancient signs and symbols.

Accessing deep wisdom that is within you, within all of us and our Earth, is part of our experiential nature. The cups are experiential, providing a starting point for retrieving social memory at any point in our lives. Think about this. Taking a cup of tea or coffee in the morning or afternoon allows us to create a contemporary space, capturing the memory embedded in our daily lives. This approach is phenomenological, meaning that it is a philosophical investigation of experience in all its varieties without reference to the objective reality of the practice. We focus solely on what we observe ourselves, not what science has shown or what others have investigated.

A cup reading is a phenomenological approach to self-awareness that allows us to reflect on:

1. The landscapes of our lives
2. How the landscapes we live in are truly experienced
3. How *we* perceive the representations and symbols in our dreams and our cups

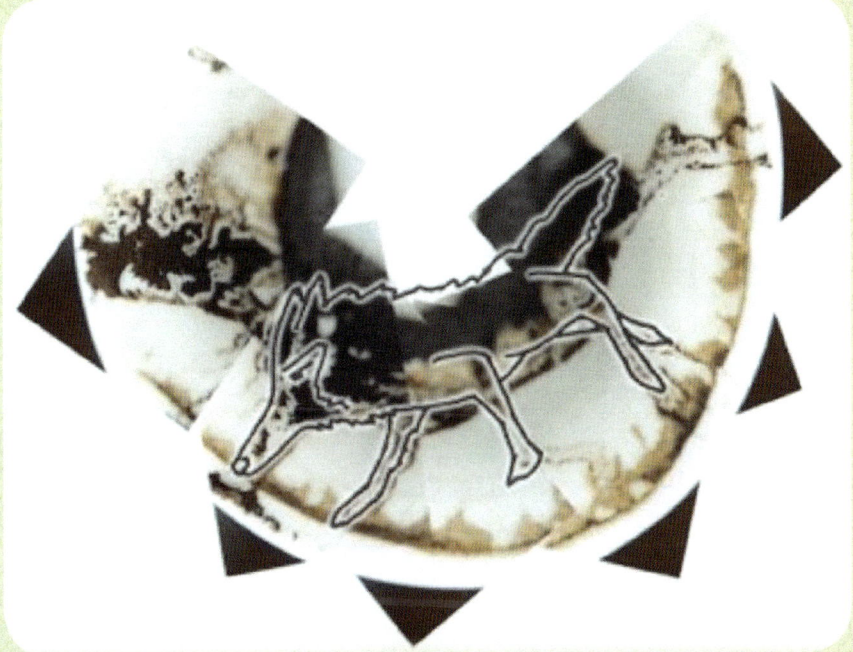

Cup with Image of a Wolf

Visual Encounters Lead to Visual Experiences: Insights for our Blindness

Our hectic lives keep us from seeing and truly experiencing the physical landscapes around us, which in turn has blinded us to our inner landscapes. Certainly, the visual encounters with the cups help us to experience life's landscapes. For example, the television's travel channel takes in places that are emotionally charged so that it etches in a living memory. We know that strong feelings lead to attachments to particular places, showing us how memory is laid down.

Blood and Honey Icons pedagogy offers an instructive view of current moments. The symbols tumbling out of the cup are a literary testimonial that lets us sample the richness of our lives. With insight, we are no longer blind. Please note that the cup reading instructions are included in the Blood and Honey Icons pedagogy information.

Artifacts of our Lives and Experiences: Clustering Symbols into Meaning

Reading and understanding the symbols and artifacts of memory is an exercise in clustering as we place the meaning of the symbols into a cohesive sentence that brings understanding. Marija Gimbutas, a renowned archaeologist, was the first in her field to develop the art of clustering symbols into meaning.

Three things to note:

1. Card and cup readings are investigations into the symbols but not fortune-telling or a search for answers.
2. The cards and cups can be used in conjunction with mnemonic techniques that reveal wisdom through the messages found in symbols and artifacts.
3. When searching for meaning, we face infinite possibilities; this raises questions rather than providing answers.

Book Template

The Blood and Honey Icons template is based on memory and the resulting oral traditions that are difficult to put on a written page. Frontier theorists ranging from quantum physics to chemistry are reviewing our ancestors' science and wisdom. According to some prominent researchers and scientists, our ancients, including women, were neither primitive nor of lower intelligence. Research, from studies to critical analysis, is being reunited with the organizing principle of Mother Nature. Information theory and the study of patterns have begun to recognize that both wisdom (information) and patterns (symbolic) create "memory."[24]

The South Slavic symbology and iconic representations in the simple kolo are both medicinal and filled with information for the body, both biological and neurological. Social scientists posit that trauma and Post Traumatic Stress Disorder are psycho-biological memory disorders with neurological features. Finally, the field of biology is opening the door to include how energy, patterns, and wisdom can guide or adapt our understanding through intricate, orchestrated responses. For example, Peter Frazer researched a system based on traditional Chinese medicine in combination with quantum wave theory to demonstrate the body's biochemistry and bio-energetics, called Nutri-Energetics or Infoceuticals. This is the same process that supports the Slavic cup readings or the I-Ching, the incorporation and integration of the psychological and the biological-soma in these ethnic cultures.

It is not a mere coincidence that most researchers I have listed here are Slavic. It follows that the research and knowledge of these phenomena would be lodged in these Slavic scientists and researchers. A.R. Luria's book *The Mind of a Mnemonist*, translated from Russian by Lynn Solotaroff, pointed to the tarot system as a mnemic instrument for monks to trigger memory through visual icons.[25] This holds true for Biosemiotics.

According to Frazer, the body processes and communicates information in its own organic way. Frazer wrote, "All these processes must be exquisitely timed, and these substances must be produced in specific quantities and delivered with precision to correct cells. It seems only reasonable to assume that this intricate biological dance must be choreographed by something. That something is information."[26] As we can see with the South Slavic and Slavic icons, symbology, and mythology, cycles of female menstruation, gestation, and daily life are acquisitively timed, as are the changes found in the seasons. In fact, the intricate biological dance referred to as the kolo for South Slavs is but a storehouse of information.

The South Slavs, with their age-old kolos and cup readings, may have practiced the oldest known form of psychology. This type of quantum wisdom is a practiced medicinal art for the body, heart, and mind. Of course, most Slavs, past and present, are unaware of these healthy chemical reactions in the body but have developed practices that honor, respect, and celebrate their culture based on the mysteries of Mother Nature, or Moist Mother Earth as the Slavs refer to Her. All that was necessary to understand is that the cups and the kolos were hubs of information that sustained the people themselves and the Earth.

Danica Anderson reading cups for Kolo Trauma Treatment, Travnik, Bosnia

Tragically for women, and for men as a result, the focus on surviving catastrophic, man-made violence has set up blockages and distortions that denigrate the female social collective that is filled with the oral memories and traditions that evolved our present society. In my present-day kolo, we are observing that Women's Cross Cultural Collaboration trauma work with South Slavic women is helping Balkan War survivors recover by reintroducing female social collective practices that were all but wiped out during the war. The information and return to Proto-Slavic female traditions were most likely triggered by crisis and trauma as opposed to ancient practices for Natural or Mother Nature disasters or catastrophes.

What I am indicating here is that most of the traumatic events were natural disasters, not manmade wars or violence, triggering their embrace of intensified learning. With manmade violence or holocaustic trauma, the embrace of intensified learning is instead an intergenerational trauma episode. The question I asked of the female war crimes survivors and war survivors in Bosnia and elsewhere was, "How would life be if we were not re-directed to female social collectives by manmade violence and trauma? What would this return look like if it were through choice at the right time but not as the result of manmade trauma?"

However, what I witnessed in the aftermath of war for these women is how the wisdom from their ancestors' past life experiences to theirs merged or became synchronized. For instance, as I talked to a woman hoeing her field or picking mountain herbs, I could have been talking to a Neolithic mother or the *Novi Travnik,* a grandmother from Bosnia-Herzegovina, reporting that her family is closer as a result of the conflict, since they have to work together in the gardens, help each other, and spend more time at the table than before the war.

Patterns of actions, behaviors, and feelings in day-to-day existence are a medicinal elixir that passes memory and wisdom down through our DNA into future generations. The South Slavs I observed did not have academic or scientific qualifications, but they did have an abundance of wisdom from generations of life experiences. The influential study of their coffee cup readings, icons, and the simple kolo round dance, age-old mnemonics and biosemiotics, revealed that the boundaries of domestic life would span many generations and cross over spatial domains. It is through the bioculinary, the cups, and their female social collective that intergenerational memories could begin to heal the survivors of catastrophic trauma. I ended up being their student, learning from the *Novi Travnik* and other Muslim women war survivors that we are embedded with information in the form of memories that engage the body's self-sustaining healing practices.

Instead of going to Bosnia to help and to heal, I went to learn from the most ancient of ancients. The body of wisdom that is in sync with biological and Earthly environs is Mother Nature kinship, sharing the wisdom everyone is born with. This is the very template that Blood and Honey follows.

Ψ Danica Anderson Ψ

Icons: Summary of Archetypal Movements

Blood and Honey Icons: Biosemiotics.

The Pedagogy of South Slavic War and War Crimes Survivors

Female Social Collective Practices

The South Slavic art of clustering meaning through archetypes, signs, and cup reading.

Hands and Feet Icon

ERIN HILLEARY

Hands & Feet

Motif

E.C.M.
Sacred journey with hands and feet a seed matrix with generative potency to access self-sustaining energy found within.

Kolo Avenue: ONE

Through archetypal and iconic methods, South Slavs have developed a mnemonic approach to preserve ancient wisdom and pass it down through the ages. For Slavs, the hand contains archetypal movements as seen through the linguistic history of the word itself. The Basque and South Slavic words for "five" come from their words for "hand" or "fist." Their words for "six" contain the root of the word "with," and their words for "seven" mean "with two more," again demonstrating the connection to the hand. Though only in Slavic does the original etymology remain, this linguistic code has passed into all Indo-European languages without the awareness of their speakers.

Big-boned and with large hands and feet, Rasema, a widow who has buried two husbands and two sons, gazes at her hands and says, "I buried my husbands and sons with these hands." Rasema slept on the graves of her sons in the Muslim graveyard outside Novi Travnik, Bosnia. "I would walk there with these feet," she says.

Sign

Research-background

Through archetypal and iconic methods, South Slavs have developed a mnemonic approach to preserve ancient wisdom and pass it down through the ages. For Slavs, the hand contains archetypal movements as seen through the linguistic history of the word itself. The Basque and South Slavic words for "five" come from their words for "hand" or "fist." Their words for "six" contain the root of the word "with," and their words for "seven" mean "with two more," again demonstrating the connection to the hand. Though only in Slavic does the original etymology remain, this linguistic code has passed into all Indo-European languages without the awareness of their speakers.

Storied Instructions

Big-boned and with large hands and feet, Rasema, a widow who has buried two husbands and two sons, gazes at her hands and says, "I buried my husbands and sons with these hands." Rasema slept on the graves of her sons in the Muslim graveyard outside Novi Travnik, Bosnia. "I would walk there with these feet," she says.

Small Acts

What have you fashioned with your hands alone that could be excavated thousands of years later, as the South Slavic archeological remains of "Old Europe" have been?

>What migrations or journeys have you undertaken mindfully in your life?

Evoking the White Birch Tree Council Icon

Evoking the White Birch Tree Council

Kolo Avenue: FOUR

Motif

E.C.M.
Matrifocal communal life orchestrated with natural organization, female social justice and compassion

Though they operated without a written alphabet, ancient Slavs had much wisdom to pass down. They were neither primitive nor uneducated; the invisible footprints of memory reveal their oral traditions, including agrarian practices and oneness with Mother Earth. Our DNA is a rich repository of South Slavic cultural wisdom.

*W*hen I learned from the, I realized I was listening to the truth of their existence.

Sign

Research-Background

Archeological evidence and research point to the Bronze Age—if not earlier—as the beginning of an ensilaged extinction and annihilation of the Earth's resources. According to studies, all of Europe and the North American continent were once covered by forests, while in the modern day, the Amazon forest is being decimated. The South Slavic love of the trees and the Moist Mother Earth is perhaps older than what has been documented since they believed in using an "invisible footprint" to leave an impact on future generations. Though they operated without a written alphabet, ancient Slavs had much wisdom to pass down. They were neither primitive nor uneducated; the invisible footprints of memory reveal their oral traditions, including agrarian practices and oneness with Mother Earth. Our DNA is a rich repository of South Slavic cultural wisdom.

In WWII-era Belarus, Russia, one of every four Belarussians was killed in the fighting. Modern versions of Russian myths and legends now incorporate a memorial architecture for those who died consisting of three birch trees in a field, with a space for the absent fourth tree to reflect the gruesome statistic.

Storied Instructions

Working with Ahmica women war crimes survivors, mostly grandmothers, meant that I would work in the fields with them before our meetings. So many times, offers to meet with them were met with the reply that they needed to attend to the fields and their livestock. When I learned from them, I realized I was listening to the truth of their existence, and only when I had sat and worked with them shoulder to shoulder could I ask if they needed help. Something about this way of being shoulder to shoulder just as it is in the round dances—the kolo—brought me closer to them.

Bioculinary

The soft wood of the white birch tree is used for broom handles and bobbins for thread, and its twigs are made into cloth. Asphyxiating gases and charcoal for gunpowder also come from the white birch tree. Russian leather products are made durable with white birch tree tar, which is also used in photography and as an insect repellant. More importantly, white birch tree tar is used in Russia in the book binding process to impede mold. The white birch tree is also used to aid in fermentation, as beer, wine, and hard liquor are made in South Slavic lands.

Sour Cabbage Sarma

This bioculinary recipe starts with a home-grown cabbage patch. Take your harvested cabbages and remove the leaves one at time. Trim the heavy vein in the leaf. Have a large glass jar cleaned and readied. Place the leaves in the glass jar and pour in home-made vinegar (clear or apple cider) with salt and water. Leave over the winter. Use the preserved cabbage in the following recipe.

Ingredients:

3 pounds of ground lamb (organic, from within 50 miles of where you live)

1 pound ground meat (organic, from within 50 miles of where you live)

or wild rice, soaked in water a day ahead of time

2 onions (organic)

salt and pepper

1/2 cup of rice if also using meat (without meat, use 2 cups)

6 cloves garlic chopped (organic, home-grown preferred)

2 large sour cabbage heads

6 tablespoons of vegetable oil

4 tablespoons flour

10 ounces of homemade tomato soup

Have the large sour cabbage leaves out on the table. Mix the meat (or rice if not using meat), chopped onion, garlic, rice, salt, and pepper together. Add a little bit of cold water. Fill cabbage leaves with mixture and roll up. Seal both ends by tucking inward. Chop up remaining head of cabbage and place in the bottom of the cauldron or kettle. Use a twelve-quart kettle. Place sarma rolls in kettle and add smoked ribs if desired. Place some chopped cabbage on top. In a sauce pan, brown the oil and add flour. Add salt and the homemade tomato soup (2 cups or 10 ounces). Bring to a boil and add to kettle of sarmas. Add more water to cover and let simmer 3 hours. Makes about 35-40 sarmas.

Small Acts

Do a circle round dance, the kolo, in a slow beat with groups that are not finding common ground, or with those whose demands are "their way or the highway – to death."

Plant a tree in the name of a woman who died from famine, gynocidal death, childbirth, or violence as a feminine reforestation campaign.

An appeal to have synchronized bleeding for three months needs to be orchestrated by women across the globe. Such an appeal would prompt evolutionary measures increasing love, honor, and respect to all females and things feminine such as the Moist Mother Earth. What if all women across the globe once a month during their menses gathered together to name the state of their feminine realities? What small acts would build into this?

Signs: Kolo Icon

Kolo Ethnochoreology

Motif

E.C.M.
Symbolically charged Literacy

Kolo Avenue: THREE

A new philology burst forth in the 1990s called the Knust-Laban Notation, or Labanotation, as researchers demanded intensive scientific methods to preserve folk dances such as the kolo.

I am not sure if it was my imagination, but their postures within their circle-kolo become erect with dignity and love for the feminine after this experience.

Sign

Research

A new philology has burst forth in the 1990s with the Knust-Laban notation (also known as *Labanotation*) as researchers demanded intensive scientific methods in preserving the kolos, or round dances. Only after serious attempts in the 1930s by two Serbian sisters, Danica and Ljubica Jankovic, the very pioneers of Serbian Ethnochoreology, was the *kolo* documented to record the pattern, rhythm, and melody of the dance steps into graphs and diagrams.

Storied Instructions

The Kolo Sumejja female Muslim war survivors from Novi Travnik, certified as kolo lay therapists, and I arranged a training and gathering with the Srebrenica Muslim women widows war crimes survivors, where almost all of their males were murdered and taken under the eyes of the Dutch military peace keeping force during the Balkan war. Coffee cups were read, and training on trauma impacts was performed. Despite the warm outreach, the spillage from an environment that seemed to contain unending war crimes narratives was absorbed by all present. The trip back to Novi Travnik from Tulza, where parts of the city are caving in due to the salt mines below, was an atmosphere of serious quiet reflection. On this trip to Belgrade, Serbia, after an invitation from a feminist activist for *The Vagina Monologues* presentation and workshop, anxiety filled the public bus ride through Bosnia-Herzegovina to Serbia. Right before Serbia, signs were posted in front of sagging and bombed homes warning us of the presence of mines. The Kolo Sumejja women were guests and afforded a stay at the hotel and the television performance of Eve Ensler's *Vagina Monologues*. The leader of Kolo Sumejja, Sana Koric, was awarded the Vagina Warrior award on television. At the *Vagina Monologues* workshop, each of the Kolo Sumejja women received a bag of condoms and other items. Returning to Novi Travnik, I begged the women to be mindful of the public bus through Serbia that our group need to take. Nisveta Dzimika Pasic is a kolo Sumejja member, a certified kolo lay therapist, and a former handball champion for the former Yugoslavia. No one can control her or tell her what to do. In the beginning of the bus ride, everything was quiet, but I noticed the bus driver whose shoulders were shaking from laughter and tears. I had too much fear to turn around to look at the former handball champion, but all the Serbs in the front of the bus did and commenced their laughter. I turned around just in time to see her blowing up a condom. She stated to me and the whole bus that she never seen a condom before, having been married to the same man all her life, and wanted to try it out. The bus slightly swerved from the convulsive laughter. I was amazed at how the former handball champion was able to be an ambassadress of peace and laughter.

For the rest of the bus ride back to Novi Travnik, she talked to everyone, saying that the "vagina" (*peechka* in Serbo-Croatian) should not be the butt of jokes or shame. Not one single person on the bus was untouched by the ironic truth of laughter that heals. After we re-entered Bosnia, the women who were raped or knew others who were raped would model the newly positive term *peechka,* as if to reclaim their female bodies. I am not sure if it was my imagination, but their postures within their circle-kolo became erect with dignity and love for the feminine after this experience.

Bioculinary

The walnut tree originated in northern Persia. The Greek names Persicon and Basilicon are related to the tree's scientific name, *regia* (royal). The walnut kernel has a close resemblance to the brain. Fishers of the sea, rivers, and lakes use walnut leaves to moisten the ground so that worms would rise to the surface for air and could be more easily collected for bait; this is an exquisite example of ethnochoreology.

Orasnica

(Nut Roll): The ultimate Ethnochoreology recipe. Recipes are the notation system for culinary arts, a form of feminine divination practicum.

Ingredients:

2 ounces compressed yeast

3 tablespoons sugar

10 tablespoons flour (Organic, stone grind by hand if possible)

4 egg yolks (nested, free range)

3 tablespoons sour cream (Organic, from cows within 50 miles of your home)

2/3 cup warm milk (Organic, from cows within 50 miles of your home)

3 cups flour (Organic, stone ground by hand if possible)

½ pound butter (Organic, from cows within 50 miles of your home)

Filling:

¾ pound ground walnuts (hand-picked from your own walnut tree if possible)

4 egg whites (free range, organic eggs, if possible from your own chickens)

1 cup sugar

Combine first four ingredients, which function as a metaphor for the four avenues of the kolo. Set aside to rise, preferably on a warm stove so that it can rise completely. Cream together butter, sugar, egg yolks, and sour cream; the elements will be integrated but retain their individual essences, which again mirrors the kolo. At this point, add the yeast mixture and flour and knead the dough for at least nine minutes. After kneading, the dough will need a lightly greased bowl where it will rise to twice its original size, like the gestating womb. Divide the dough into thirds: the triple aspect, Maiden, Mother, and Crone. Roll it (much like the round dances, or kolos) into a rectangular shape and fill the center of the rectangular shape of dough with walnut filling (*see recipe below*). Place in a 13" x 9" pan for one hour on a warm stove (*pech* in Serbo-Croatian) to allow the dough to rise and gestate again with its walnut filling and chant loving thoughts while waiting. (The walnut filling is the mitochondrial DNA metaphor, a tree ring record.)

Place into the oven (*the pech,* which is the womb) at 350 degrees (in numerology, we add the numerals in 350 to get 8, the number for eternity).

To make the filling, beat egg whites, add sugar and ground walnuts. Do not allow the filling to become stiff; if this happens, simply add a small portion of warm milk (recall breastmilk nourishing a child as you do this).

Small Acts

The *kolo* round dances for South Slavs are the notation system of our genes and Mother Nature's evolutionary practices. Requiring a different alphabet and language that included the feminine and not excluding the masculine or children, the round dances held harmonic bonds with the Moist Mother Earth. The signs and the inscriptions speak of how to include the environment, the landscapes of Moist Mother Earth, into intelligence. Already, we now know in biology that cells are clearly "intelligent" when grouped together.

What have you collected in life? Those who gather together to enact or effect change seek the wisdom of circles, of groups such as those who dance the kolo. Signs and inscriptions offer an invitation to group collective consciousness that is seriously missing from ordinary lectures, marches, and concert halls.

If you were to employ Ethnochoreology to your life now, what signs or inscriptions would most express and convey your first person story?

Bogumile: Green Man, Thunder God

Ψ Danica Anderson Ψ

Bogumile- Green Man- Thunder God

Kolo Avenue: TWO

Motif

Wounding

E.C.M.
Honor, Protection of Feminine, Ritual practice as learning tool

The Bogumiles were known to practice the holy Pagan mysteries of the Lost Goddess, an oral memory tradition practiced by South Slavs for millennia.

*T*he Green Man legends appear in his life as his friends spoke of his looking for new green shoots of plant life on the very spot of his dismemberment.

Sign Praying

Research

early Paulist Christians practiced their reverence of Moist Mother Earth, which was the creed of the Bogumiles. After two hundred years of denying Jesus as divine, the Bogumile kings were slaughtered in the tenth century by the Pope's armies, leaving standing stones as a haunting memorial. The very literal, who are unable to understand the wisdom of myths, icons, symbols, and archetypes, especially those in the Christian church, dedicated themselves to the eradication of the Bogumiles. The Bogumiles were known to practice the holy Pagan mysteries of the Lost Goddess, referring to the hidden love and honor for the Great Mother deity supplanted by patriarchs, which is an oral memory tradition practiced by South Slavs that is for millennia. The Knights Templar and the Masons received instructions from the Bogumiles, but both all-male cults exploited and manipulated the Lost Goddess instructions and their respective icons and, instead of revering the feminine as they had been taught, committed gender violence.

Storied Instructions

A Muslim war survivor from Novi Travnik, Bosnia, who was left paralyzed and in a wheelchair somehow crawled up into the surrounding, heavily treed, mountainous foothills and carefully detonated his stash of grenades. Completely dismembered just as in Dionysian mythologies, the paraplegic war survivor took his life near the time of the fall equinox. The Green Man legends appear in his life as his friends spoke of his looking for new, green shoots of plant life on the very spot of his dismemberment.

Bioculinary

Associated with the Plant Gladiska (Ononis spinosa L.), Restharrow is used for the kidneys and has a foul smell. It emits this odor when farmers attempt to remove it from the soil. Restharrow is a wild licorice, and its roots are used for rheumatism and gout. The plant has tenacious roots into the Moist Mother Earth. Growing to between one and two feet, the plant's posture mirrors the Bogumile standing stones and their totem, the oak tree. The following recipe is called Bosanski Lonac.

Bosanski Lonac

(*Lonac* is cauldron and or pot in Serbo-Croatian)

Ingredients:

2 ½ pounds White Northern Beans or 4 pounds lamb cut in pieces (organic, from within 150 miles of residence)

1 green pepper cut in large pieces

5 large yellow potatoes

2 hot chili peppers

1 head of cabbage cut into 8 pieces

3 tomatoes

3 carrots cut in one-inch pieces

1 pound string beans

1 stalk celery, diced

2 heads of garlic, unpeeled salt to taste

30 peppercorns

fresh lemon juice and water

Select a *lonac* (stewing kettle or cauldron, which abound in Bosnia) that can contain the layering of the food stuff as follows:

Put lamb pieces as one layer and vegetables as another until no more ingredients remain. This culinary action represents the Bogumile-Green Men legends, which are connected by themes of dismemberment and connecting the pieces of fragmented lives into one family.

Add the fresh lemon juice and water to the *lonac,* covering the ingredients with two inches of water. Seal with an airtight lid, or alternatively, use a pressure cooker pot. If no sealed lid is available, seal with aluminum foil and do not open until done. Shake the *lonac* like you would popcorn every 15 minutes to prevent burning. Cook over low to medium heat for at least 2 ½ hours.

Small Acts:

Make a list of what actions or words enacted are questionable. Make a list of your actions and words that may be questionable. Make a list of actions that you did not perform and what what would have happened if each had been carried out.

Write responses for each of your lists based on your future actions. Write what you will do or what you envision doing to bring about change in your life. Consider the input or stimuli that you will act on and the actions that you will perform as a result.

Storied Aprons

Storied Aprons

Kolo Avenue: TWO

Motif

E.C.M.
Connects to progressive doubling, pregnancy, abundance, and the power of two

South Slavic storied aprons are the first person stories of daughters, mothers, and grandmothers handed down through mitochondrial DNA and into future generations.

*T*heir aprons are often stained with blood which became a patina of emblazoned copper despite the rigors of laundry done by wide Slavic hands.

Sign

Research

The apron is a proud representative of the textile and weaving arts; it should not be debased simply because of its connection to housework. The weaving of the cloth itself and the observance that females across the globe still perform most domestic labor recommends the practice of honoring a female's capacity to manifest culture, as these arts bring life and regeneration. The apron suggests a necklace adorning the womb/uterus. The South Slavic ancient baba (wise women in Serbo-Croatian) apron honors destiny and the fates in the rich soup found in the cauldron of life. South Slavic storied aprons are the first person stories of daughters, mothers, and grandmothers handed down through mitochondrial DNA and into future generations.

Storied Instructions

The Bosnian Muslim Ahmici grandmothers who survived the massacre and other war crimes of April 16, 1994, were in the field with the cows and the land during that early morning hour. Their aprons are often stained with blood, which became a patina of emblazoned copper despite the rigors of laundry done by wide South Slavic hands.

Bioculinary

An oak Yule log is burned on January 6th, a practice still found in the Serbian Orthodox Church but also in the rural areas of former Yugoslavia. The oral memory tradition of burning the oak log is noted in many prehistoric anthropology and archeological artifacts. Instead of the evergreen tree dressed in ornaments, the hard wood oak was burned in sacrifice to coax the sun to return for spring and summer crops.

Small Acts

Place in your pocket, preferably an apron pocket, symbolic and representative pictures, items that are to be passed down through the generations.

Porodin Dwelling Domovi (Home/Temple)

CONNIE SIMPSON

Porodin Dwelling
Domovi (Home/Temple)

Motif

E.C.M.
A seed matrix with the generative potency to access self-sustaining energy found within.

Kolo Avenue: ONE

Ancient dwellings, or domovi in Serbo-Croatian, have revealed artifacts from 6,000 BCE demonstrating the prevalence of Bird Goddess worship.

All involved asked that I keep my vow to speak their stories.

Sign

Research

The *domovi* is the home, specifically the residence of the ancestors. Artifacts from a *domovi* dating from 6,000 BC appear to have been used in the worship of the Bird Goddess. One artifact depicts a Bird Goddess as the chimney, decorated with collars and necklaces.[1] A *domovi* near a girl's grave at Azod, north of Budapest, incorporates a bird head elevated on a massive human leg; another artifact of a domovi was found in Porodin-Pelagonia near Bitolj in the former Yugoslavia and dates from the 6th or 7th millennium BC. Each domovi artifact has a chimney with a zoomorphic Bird Goddess at the peak. She has T-shaped eyebrows, and the homes themselves have inverted T-shaped (upside-down upper case T) entrances.

Storied Instructions

I write only the stories of those who have given me permission to share the events of their lives in this book, though some of the names have been changed. All involved asked that I keep my vow to speak their stories, and this book is a result of my commitment to them. My experiences with the women and their cup readings are all a narrative of first person stories finding their way into this book.

When asked why she and her family did not leave before the Balkan war broke out, Sana responded that she and her two sons were to go to relatives in America. Her husband would not go but would keep the house guarded. Looking intently at the sky, Sana spoke of having an intuitive feeling that if she left with her two sons, her husband would be killed. Instead of leaving for safe ground, Sana and her two sons decided to stay together in their home.

Bioculinary

Lanilist (Toadflax) is associated with the home because the mouth of the flower is sealed shut until a honeybee works to open the entrance with its long tongue. The orange flower attracts the desired guests. The interior of the flower is in the form of a cave with egg-shaped seed vessels. Toads are known to sit beneath the flower, which is used as an astringent, hepatic, and detergent. The following recipe is for a dish called *koljivo*. It is best to use all organic ingredients that come from within 150 miles of your residence.

Koljivo

Ingredients:
1 pound wheat grain
1 tablespoon pure vanilla
1 pound sugar
2 tablespoons rum
1 pound walnuts, ground
½ cup water

Take 2 rounded tablespoons of sugar and ground walnuts to set aside for the topping of the Koljivo.

Cook wheat in clear water over medium heat. Add your blessings and mantras to the water and boiling process by singing or speaking them aloud. Change the water several times during the boiling process and replace it with cold water. Once wheat is cooked, drain completely and place it on a clean cloth to dry. Grind the wheat. As you grind the wheat, express your gratitude and what you love.

Mix wheat, sugar, walnuts, vanilla, and rum. Add water until mixture is moist but not wet. Place the mixture on a beautiful serving platter and shape it into a kolo, a round Moist Mother Earth form. Decorate with the sugar and walnuts that were set aside. Serve this on ritual occasions requiring honor, respect, and grace.

Small Acts

Look about your home right now. Take photos of each room and the outside along with the yard. Bring them to work, or circle of friends that have not seen your home ask them what they see in the photos. Is it a place that they would want to seek and rest in? Ask your family members what they see in each photograph of the home. Most importantly, what do you see with your heart and spirit?

Do their responses hold rejuvenation, respect and sanctuary descriptions? If not, where do you seek rejuvenation and sanctuary? Are there proscribed female roles in the home amongst family members? Is there domestic violence in verbal and emotional mood swings from family members in the sanctuary? Is there respect for the matriarch and females in the home, or do the females own every single unmitagating unending task while the males do weekly, monthly chores only?

Mother Tongue: Spirituality of Relatedness and Connectivity

Mother Tongue
spirituality of connectiveness & relatedness

Kolo Avenue: TWO

Motif

E.C.M.
Pro-social intelligence language with responses of rituals and traditions. The organic phenomenon of the universe reflecting a limitless creative intelligence

A passion for eternal truth, awe, and curiosity. Cooking up creation, even in the prenatal dimension, where science has demonstrated the ability of the fetus to learn inside the womb, responding to music and reacting to the voices of family after birth.

*T*he round dances (kolos) and the chanting songs sung by the women working in the fields and at the hearth have preserved South Slavic female humanity and the Mother Tongue into our modern era.

Sign

Research

South Slavs have archaic traditions rooted in oration; they were able to recite myths, stories, and songs that contained thousands of lines of poetry and narrative. South Slavs did not have a written alphabet until the late 1800s, but instead used mnemonic devices to ingrain their oral tradition into their memories. The round dances—kolos—along with the chanting songs sung by the women working in the fields and at the hearth preserved Slavic female culture and the Mother Tongue right into our modern era. Rhythm and melody transmitted female wisdom in the prosodic recitation of the Mother Tongue.

Storied Instructions

In Travnik, Bosnia, the most beautiful town in all of Bosnia-Herzegovina, mother to the factory town of Novi Travnik, a group of internally displaced refugees huddled in a dilapidated gymnasium more than ten years after the war. Electricity was turned off by the municipality, making the search for firewood a life and death priority. When the *Kolo Sumejja* women came with their huge bags of flour, oil, milk, cheese, and juice, the refugees were profoundly moved. At the end of the gathering with the Travnik refugees, a cassette tape was played. An old kolo round dance song sliced through the air as we all danced the steps out of the cold and filthy gymnasium whose foul smell had been seeping into our pores. The women refugees were crying and said that they had not heard that song since before the war; it was a forgotten language.

Bioculinary

The oak tree represents the Slavic Secret Language, a language of symbols and iconic representations like a picture speaking a thousand words; the term also allows for a vast diversity of iconic associations that is in harmony with Mother Nature.

Powered oak bark mixed with honey heals menstrual problems. A blend of ground acorns mixed with water treats diarrhea. The mixture of acorns and oak bark milk is an antidote to poisonous herbs. This recipe is for Czarska. or Queen's Torte.

The nine-ounce Czarska, or Queen's Lenten Torte, is often baked during Lent and is a very old bioculinary recipe that must have been made at the vernal equinox and winter solstice for thousands of years.

As with all bioculinary recipes, home-grown, local, and seasonal ingredients are preferred.

Czarska

Ingredients:

9 ounces of ground walnuts

1 teaspoon baking powder

9 ounces sugar

1½ cups of pure or artesian well water

9 ounces of organic flour

3 tablespoons of homemade organic jam

4 tablespoons of bread crumbs

In a bowl, combine all ingredients except the jam. Mix thoroughly, considering how this activity signifies the interconnectivity of female lives. Pour half of the batter into a well-greased, 9-inch cake pan. Spread the jam over the batter. Pour the last half of the batter over the jam. Place in a 350-degree oven and bake for 45 minutes, which in numerology is known as (4 + 5= 9). Since 9 is a factor of 3, and 3 is the troika for Slavs, most Slavs note the importance of bioculinary arts and these parameters for even baking time as being synchrony, therefore in harmony with Mother Nature.

Small Acts

Choose a symbol for each decade of life to represent your most significant life experiences of that decade. Choose a picture of yourself in each decade of life and write on the back of the photograph: "Once upon a time…" and then fill in your first-person story. Take the photograph with your first person story and make it into postcards. Discover the people in your life that would receive a postcard.

Maternal Fright: The Eye of Memory and Repression of Female Genealogies

Maternal Fright

Motif

E.C.M.
passion for eternal truths, awe, curiosity. Cooking up creation even in the prenatal dimension where it is known that fetuses learn inside the

Kolo Avenue: TWO

To grow, evolve, gestate.

*W*hat the mother feels or is emotionally exposed to will be expressed in the fetus, both physically and mentally.

Sign

Research

Psychiatrist Dr. Lloyd DeMause chronicles what South Slavic wise women already knew: When a mother lives in fright, there are consequences for her and for all others in the community. According to DeMause, children who survive their mothers' maternal fright during pregnancy have increased aggressiveness, personality disorders, attention-deficit complications, and other physiological effects. Perinatal psychology and somatic psychology view the womb as an intensive, collaborative learning mode and environment within the body of the mother. What the mother feels or is emotionally exposed to will be expressed in the fetus, both physically and mentally.

Storied Instructions

When I was in Bosnia in 2003, I discovered that the word trauma in Serbo-Croatian means to wound and to rub or turn. I watched Semka's constant rubbing of her swollen belly with affection while twinges of angst appeared in her shaking hands. Our psychological being sustains substantial and lasting damage over time, as noted in various pathologies such as PTSD, or what I call Manmade Trauma. Her husband lost eighteen relatives in the Ahmica-Vittez war crimes on April 16, 1993. Semka feared her unborn child had encoded the fear and her maternal fright in DNA and that this would manifest in possible illnesses as the child develops.

Bioculinary

The silver linden tree has a rounded pyramid shape resembling the vulva, with extremely fragrant flowers in summer bursting through the air with the scents of lime and carob. The blossoms and fruit are oval and used in France to make Tilleul Tea. Silver linden is known for its herbal properties to aid sleep and indigestion. The linden tree often grows near oak trees.

This recipe is for egg bread, a traditional Slavic bread usually baked at the vernal equinox.

Egg Bread

2 packages active dry yeast
1 tablespoon salt
½ cup warm water
3 eggs

1-1/2 cups lukewarm milk, scalded
¼ cup softened butter or ghee
7 to 7 ½ cups flour
¼ cup sugar

Dissolve the yeast in warm water. Stir in all ingredients except 3½ cups of the flour. Beat until smooth. Mix in the enough remaining flour to make the dough pliable and easy to knead. Turn the dough on a lightly floured board. Knead until shiny and smooth like a baby's skin. Grease a bowl and place the dough into it. Rub oil on the dough, cover, and let it rise until it doubles in size. Punch down the dough. Divide in half to form two loaves. Place seam side down in two greased nine-inch loaf pans. Cover and let the dough rise until double, usually about an hour. Bake 25 to 30 minutes at 375 degrees.

If you are pregnant, bake the egg bread during each month of your pregnancy. If you are trying to become pregnant, make the egg bread when you are ovulating. If you are menopausal, bake the egg bread on the date of your birth each month of the year. The kneading of the dough is a metaphor for moving through maternal fright, and making the dough shiny and smooth as a baby's bottom signifies a female's ability to give birth and manifest the intangible. Punching the dough signifies punching through fear and violence into new possibilities. The double rising of the bread dough shows the possibility of abundance and the "pregnancy" of the creative process.

Small Acts

Create small acts that dispel maternal fright for you and pregnant women. Begin with your own fears, list each time you have a fear or use fear in your words. The danger is more real when we realize how we live in fear, sleep in fear and think in fear.

We are learning from South Slavic women who are seasoned with maternal fright by wars and violence where they dwell—both the home and the womb. When have you asked a gestating mother what would make her feel safe for herself and her unborn child?

Ψ BLOOD & HONEY Ψ

Weaver-Spinner Icon

Weaver-Spinner

Kolo Avenue: THREE

Motif

E.C.M.
Designs of an ancient system to express what cannot be seen but known

Weaving is the aesthetic artistic expression of the "Old Europe" Bird Goddess — Baba Yaga Folklore symbolic system and ideology of female culture.

*L*iving perpetually in the "land of they", the Novi Travnik, Bosnian *stara Baba* in her victim hood and blame cannot weave another tapestry or spin new life for her grandchildren.

Sign

Research

In Southeastern Europe, the center of "Old Europe" (6500 BCE-3500BCE), the loom was located next to the altar to fashion ceremonial clothing "indicating that the process of weaving itself must have a sacred meaning… the earliest evidence goes back to the 7th millennium BCE."[2] Weaving is the aesthetic artistic expression of the "Old Europe" Bird Goddess, or Baba Yaga, whose mythology and symbolic representations are iconic of female culture.

Storied Instructions

Invited for tea one afternoon, I had barely sat down in the incredibly clean house when the elderly woman brought out the remains of her hand-embroidered linens. The *stara Baba* described how "they" had urinated, vomited, and stomped on her linen work, which was now stained beyond repair. Over forty years of exquisite hand work and loom work was violated, and now the stara Baba no longer does her weaving or sewing.

Bioculinary

Wild Bilberry, or borovica, is rare in the United States but prevalent in Bosnia. It is known for improving nearsightedness, increasing capillary strength, and aiding digestion. This recipe is for South Slavic Corn Bread.

The round *pech* (stove or oven), an archeological legacy of Neolithic ancients, bakes bread to its fullest potential. Build an outdoor beehive oven for this recipe with your own hands. Grow your own corn and grind it into cornmeal.

South Slavic Corn Bread

Ingredients:

5 cups of organic corn meal

5 eggs (free range and preferably your own)

1 teaspoon salt

2 cups organic milk

1 cup Crisco (vegan substitute for lard)

Sift cornmeal with salt and add Crisco, eggs, and one cup of milk. Weave in and out of the mixture for 15 minutes. Add the remaining milk. Pour into a greased 13"x 9" baking dish and bake at 375 degrees. When it is getting to a golden color, immediately remove from oven. Cut into squares and return pan to oven to complete baking. Total baking time is 50 to 60 minutes. South Slavs serve this bread warm with warm cheese or sour cream.

Small Acts

The weavers are imbued with the ability to create universes. Known as "biocentrism" current western science and quantum physics posit that "the universe is created by life and not the other way around, " (Robert Lanza, Bob Berman, The Biocentric Universe, Discover, May 2009) scientists only now understand the ancient women's weaving symbols and archetypes of how we are the creators and destroyers of life.

Do you intimately know your essence? Or do you live in the land of "they"?

Do you dress according to your essence or according to the fashion dictates?

What would your wardrobe say of your essence?

What would your linens, fabrics and even kilns express?

What symbols or patterns predominant your fabrics and clothing or pottery?

Tree Spirits: Vila, or the Witch

Tree Spirits Vila-Witch

Motif

E.C.M.
surrendering to sacred energies, connecting to all living things such as animal totems or other spirit bodies

Kolo Avenue: TWO

The Vili (sing. Vila) are fairy witches (Vjestica in Serbo-Croatian). The numerous classifications of the Slavic dryads and tree spirits are exclusively female pointing to how language originated from a mother/sister kinship expression. For instance there are the wood fairy witches (Sumska Vila) and the Vodena Vila (water nymphs), Mala Vila (Little or Pixy) and Brodarica Villa (Undine).

"*My* grandmother told me it is the end of world if a grandmother dies alone."

Sign

Research

The etymology of the word *Serb* is unknown, which underscores its ancient, prehistoric origins. Tracing the variants of the word Serb reveals that one close relation is Sarmatian, a word of Iranian origin whose root is *sary,* meaning cypress tree. This identifies a kinship between the word Serb and the forest. The Serbo-Croatian word *srkati,* meaning to suck in, refers to drinking and even sharing mother's milk, as in nursing. Marija Gimbutas' archeological research points to the Old Russian and Serbo-Croatian words for *Baba Yaga* as referring to an old woman or a pelican; *yaga,* a word that derives from the word *yega,* meaning sickness or death, means fear or wrath.[3] These word origins refer to prehistoric mythologies of the Goddesses of Rejuvenation and Death, the origins of witches, who are demonized in the modern day.

Storied Instructions

Her room was stuffed to above the tall school windows with the clothes and garbage of other refugees. As a result, cockroaches crawled over her bedding, which was piled with many blankets as she talked with me. Gravely ill, she spoke of being a diabetic and having kidney failure. At best, she might have might have a few weeks of life left.

Bioculinary

The silver linden tree, or *serbrena lipa* in Serbo-Croatian, has dense foliage and is native to Southeastern Europe. The dense foliage does not allow undergrowth, and the fruit has hairs growing from the bulb. The hair represents the silver mane of the *Midday Vila,* a Slavic mythology feature and portrait of a hag or Baba Yaga-Mother Nature for Slavs. The following recipe is for *palachinke,* or dessert pancakes.

All ingredients should be organic, grown within 150-mile radius of your home, and/or hand-produced as much as possible.

Palachinke

1 quart milk
Grated rind of 1 lemon
2 heaping tablespoons of lard (may substitute coconut oil)
Cottage cheese or jelly, depending on your preference
1 teaspoon of salt
Cream, as needed for batter
2 eggs
Sugar, to taste and preference
1 cup plus 2 teaspoons organic flour

Melt lard (or coconut oil) and add to milk, then add in cream and remaining ingredients and beat the ingredients until batter is smooth. Pour a small amount of batter on a preheated, greased griddle or frying pan. When edges begin to brown lightly, turn over the pancake and brown the other side. The process of browning allows the discipline of listening to the midday Vila for an hour.

As the pancakes become done, place on a large platter. Spoon cottage cheese or jelly on each pancake. Roll and place in an oblong glass baking dish side by side. Pour sweet cream over the top and sprinkle with sugar. Bake at 350 degrees for 30 minutes.

Small Acts

Your quest is to plan an hour's worth of expression- your beliefs, values and wisdom you have lived. Reflect on how your grandmothers died—was it with grace and dignity? Who was there to witness their deaths and listen for an hour?

Creatively design a collective archive of the truth unsaid (you have three billion years of evolution) to instigate a collective social movement or support a social movement.

Lastly, have ever witnessed a tree falling in the forest? If not, plan to create opportunities to not just hear a tree fall but to witness the tree falling.

Young Maiden Midday and Lady of Midnight

Young Maidens Midday & Lady Midnight

Kolo Avenue: TWO

Motif

E.C.M.
Awe-filled respect for the Moist Mother Earth and Mother Nature, known as Baba Yaga.

Psezpolnica is the young maiden in Serbo-Croatian; she is about twelve-years-old and is associated with midday. *Poluden*, the word for noon, is associated with the highest summer temperatures. *Polunoenica*, the Lady of Midnight, is known for her long, sagging breasts that reach to her stomach. She often appears as Baba Yaga, The Widow Goddess, or Mother Nature.

She said this lack of words is `uvreda.' Uvreda means wounding.

Sign

Research

Often associated with events in which children have gone missing during the hot summer months in the former Yugoslavia, in recent centuries, *Pszpolnica* is blamed for children lost in fields and forests. The mythology shows the influence of the strong, illuminating midday sun. Tracing the references to *Pszpolnica* is a path in Slavic prehistory oral memory traditions. First, we investigate the origins of the *Pszpolnica*. *Pszpolnica* in Serbo-Croatian is the Young Maiden of the Midday; twelve years of age, she represents the twelve planets that can be seen during the day. The word for noon, *poluden,* refers etymologically to the notion that *Pszpolnica* appears only when it is the hottest summer temperature possible. *Polunocnica,* Lady of the Midnight, is known for her long, sagging breasts hanging to her stomach and crone appearance as Baba Yaga, also known as Mother Nature, or the Widow Goddess. She is thought to be the third sister of Zorya, one of the guardians of the wolf that, if is loosed upon the world, will destroy anything in its path. Another association from prehistory is the Egyptian Goddess Sekhmet, also known as the noon sun.

Storied Instructions

She is a seventy-six-year-old war crimes survivor with missing teeth; it is clear that the "bite" has gone out of her as she walks me around her property. She is constantly smoking as if to commit a slow suicide from her guilt of surviving war crimes on top of this. The widow barely eats despite the large quantity of vegetables from her garden. The foundation of her former house was the only thing visible after the scorching fire from grenades on April 16th, 1993. Now, a row of corn and masses of healthy vegetables fill the entire outline of the cement ruins in the noonday sun.

Bioculinary

Horseradish, or *hren*, is used in Southern Europe for making schnapps. It did not become a widely used flavoring or spice in Europe until the 16th century. It is known for its medicinal properties to heal bronchitis and infections. The following recipe is for *rahatlokum*, a Bosnian confection similar to Turkish Delight made from starch and sugar.

Rahatlokum

4 cups granulated sugar

1¼ cups cornstarch

1 teaspoon cream of tartar

4¼ cups water

1 tablespoon lemon juice

1½ tablespoons rosewater

1 cup confectioners' sugar

Vegetable oil or shortening

Grease the sides and bottom of a nine-inch baking dish with vegetable oil or shortening. Line with wax paper and grease the wax paper. Combine lemon juice, sugar, and 1½ cups water in a small saucepan on medium heat. Stir constantly until sugar dissolves. Allow mixture to boil. Reduce heat to low and allow to simmer. Use a candy thermometer to determine when the mixture reaches 240 degrees. Remove from heat and set aside.

Combine cream of tartar, 1 cup corn starch, and remaining water in saucepan over medium heat. Stir until all lumps are gone and the mixture begins to boil. Stop stirring when the mixture thickens. Stir in the lemon juice, water, and sugar mixture.

Stir constantly for about 5 minutes. Reduce heat to low and allow to simmer for 1 hour, stirring frequently.

Once the mixture has become a golden color, stir in rosewater. Pour mixture into lined baking dish. Spread evenly and allow to cool overnight, through the midnight hours. The next day at midday, sift together confectioner's sugar and remaining cornstarch. Turn over baking pan onto clean counter or table and tap lightly to release. Cut into one-inch pieces with oiled knife. Coat with confectioner's sugar mixture. Serve immediately or store in airtight container in layers separated with wax or parchment paper.

Small Acts

With the catastrophic violence against females, women are often coached, counseled in ways of protecting themselves from rape, assault, domestic violence but not for war crimes. This lays blame on the female and all her relations to include men and sentient beings. How would the world be if we instead ask, "What does this catastrophic violence mean to you?" What if we invited women to speak the violences visited upon them and we responded?

Ask someone each day and truly listen.

The Bear Goddess, The Madonna Goddess, and The Bird Goddess: The Many Faces of the Goddess and Her Unifying Hidden Force

Bear Madonna

Kolo Avenue: TWO

Motif

E.C.M.
Possessing an underlying solidarity, revealing many ways to begin and end.

The Bear is the fierce protectress of the young, hence her association with Mother Earth.

I was compelled to reflect on what would make her leave behind a young child and husband and wondered whether if she need to fly like the Bird Goddesses do.

Sign

Research

A clay artifact from the early Vinca period found in the former Yugoslavia reveals the significance of the Bear-Madonna Goddess to early Slavs. This clay altar table features a masked, female animal that clearly represents the ever-changing nature of the goddess. The bull horns decorating the table are associated with the sacred horns of the goddess since they have the archetypal shape of the uterus and fallopian tubes, while the bear elements reflect her aspect of the fierce protectress of the young, hence her connection to Mother Earth.

Storied Instructions

In Novi Travnik and Travnik, Bosnia, in the aftermath of the war, the women, mostly younger mothers, were leaping out their flat windows or off their minuscule balconies. With no community among women because of the nature of the neighbor-on-neighbor violence, including torture, rape, and murder, friendship among refugees simply did not occur. I walked around a mortar-cracked shell of an apartment building and passed the loads of wood piled higher than the Bosnian snowdrifts to where one young woman had leaped to her death. A handmade broom haunted the very spot where she had fallen. I was compelled to reflect on what would make her leave behind a young child and husband and wondered whether if she needed to fly like the Bird Goddesses do.

Bioculinary

The semi-wild plum tree, known in Bosnia as the *Pozegaca*, is grown entirely from seed. Fermented, it makes a whiskey called *šljivovica*. In Albania-Lepushe, bordering Serbia and Montenegro, Prunus domestica L.-Rosaceae is used to make compresses for chest colds and wounds and is poured into children's ears for earaches.

The following directions are for a traditional Bosnian chai tea (*slatko*) with plum jam and double cream (*kymak*).

Bosnian Chai Tea with Plum Jam and Double Cream

If you can, travel to the mountains of Bosnia or search for a local source for these ingredients. Hand-pick your plants and flowers for teas, working with women who know the herbs and plants. Return home and brew your cup of tea.

Some plants you might find include Basil (Ocimum basilicum), Arnica Montana (also known as leopard's bane, wolf's bane, mountain tobacco, and mountain arnica), Wild Thyme (Thymus serpyllum), and Peppermint (mentha piperita).

Grow your plums or go to an orchard within a local radius during mid- September. To locate the right seeds or orchard, look for the ecotype Prunusinsistitia, or *pozegaca* in Bosnian. Grown entirely from seed, the plum trees are semi-wild.

Pick the plums when they are fully ripe to make peeling them easier. Wash them and drop in boiling water. Remove the pit with a sewing needle. Soak the plums in lime and water. Boil with lemon slices in clear sugar syrup. Add in walnuts for aphrodisiac properties. Place in canning jars.

To make *kaymak,* first locate a dairy or organic farm and purchase organic milk. Boil milk slowly, simmering for two hours over low heat. Turn off the heat, skim off the cream, and chill for several days.

Small Acts

When guests arrive in your home, serve the tea, jam, and kaymak.

Broom: The Spiritual Practice and Art of Divination

Broom: The Art of Divination

Kolo Avenue: ONE

Motif

E.C.M.
Transforming what is ordinary into the extraordinary.

The Slavic World Tree represents the ancestors nesting in the branches, with its roots fed by the Moist Mother Earth, its trunk the great pillar or sacred mountain, the highest branch pointing toward the North Star. The North Star (*Danica*) is iconic of truth and the path between worlds, manifesting great wisdom and depth. The North Star recalls the World Tree, both of which represent the path that leads us to enlightenment. The broom is handmade from trees and is used as totem identification.

Sign

Research

The Slavic World Tree represents the ancestors nesting in the branches, with its roots fed by the Moist Mother Earth, its trunk the great pillar or sacred mountain, the highest branch pointing toward the North Star. The North Star (*Danica*) is iconic of truth and the path between worlds, manifesting great wisdom and depth. "Though the celestial reflection or correspondence of the 'central pivot' is most often said to be the North Star, the World Tree or road that leads us there usually finds its astronomical counterpart in the Milky Way. The Balts and Slavs, like most ancient European peoples, perceived their natural environment as a microcosm of the great universe; hence the celestial river Daugava was also a real physical river now known as the Dvina River in former Yugoslavia." Kenneth Johnson, Slavic Sorcery: Shamanic Journey of Initiation.

Storied Instructions

Only a few kilometers from Novi Travnik, in the year 2000, a young family returned to their farm. The mother had a small toddler still being breastfed as her husband and twelve-year-old daughter went to plow the fallow field. The landmines awaited her daughter and husband, killing the father instantly. The daughter died an agonizing death, screaming, when she could, her plea for immediate death. One Travnik woman at the bus stop discussed the incident with her friend, saying that she now feels a need to sweep and clean up the carnage for the mother and son.

Bioculinary

The European chestnut tree grows at the edges of meadows from Southern Europe to Asia. The chestnut is picked in autumn. The bark contains narcotic and febrifuge properties and is used as a tonic. The large leaves are iconic of the hand and fingers, and when the chestnut falls, it is split into three valves—the wall of a seed pod and other fruit that splits apart effortlessly to reveal its contents. During winter, the tender buds are defended by fourteen scales and gummed shut with a sticky substance so that the icy weather does not damage the bud. The sticky resin melts in the first warm days of spring. The chestnuts are said to be effective in the treatment of rheumatism, neuralgia, and rectal problems.

The Siberian silver birch tree, located in Russia and northern Asia, produces seed so abundantly that it appears to be in powder form. It is known as a pioneer species, as it is the first tree species to grow in land after the glaciers recede and offers protection to oak trees, which helps to nurture forest growth. Early pollen records from the Holocene Era suggest that the Betula species of trees heralded the post-Ice Age warming period. These trees are also the most likely source of the first brooms and are used to make charcoal, compost, dye, fiber, fungicide, paper, insect repellent, furniture polish, tanning, roof thatching, and waterproofing. The bark can be removed without killing the tree and can be used to make drinking vessels, canoe skins, and roofing tiles, among many other things. The wood and bark are waterproof, durable, tough, and resinous. The supple branches and twigs, used to make kitchen whisks and fire beaters, are known to be the materials that comprise besoms, or "witches' brooms."

The Siberian silver birch tree also has many edible parts, including its flowers, inner bark, leaves, and sap. The inner bark can be cooked or dried and ground into a meal; it is then used as a thickener for soups and puddings and mixed in with flour for bread. The inner bark is generally only seen as a famine food, used when other forms of starch are not available or are in short supply.[4] A tea is made from the leaves and another tea is made from the essential oil in the inner bark. When sunny conditions set in after a heavy frost, the sap has a sweet flavor. Birch tree wine is said to cure kidney stones and skin disease.

The Siberian silver birch's medicinal properties include anticholesterolemic, anti-inflammatory, antirheumatic, antiseptic, astringent, cholagogue, diaphoretic, diuretic, laxative, and lithontripic. The bark itself can be used as a diuretic and laxative. An oil obtained from the inner bark is astringent and is used in the treatment of various skin afflictions, especially eczema and psoriasis.

The following recipe of for kesten pile'ca supa, or chestnut-chicken soup.

Kesten Pile'ca Supa

Ideally, grow two chestnut trees from seeds for pollination purposes. Raise chickens or procure free-range organic chickens. Use the chicken bones for making stock and the eggs for this soup. If you grow and raise your own ingredients, this recipe can take five to ten years to complete.

Grow celery and onions to use in the recipe or buy local, organic produce. Use a wooden butter churn and wooden spoons fashioned by your own hands or those of other craftspersons. When making chestnut purée, use a wooden hand masher as opposed to metal or an electric food processor.

In a soup pan, melt 1 teaspoon butter and then add in 1 tbsp flour, stirring until smooth. Pour in 2 cups of chestnut purée, 2 cups of milk, 6 cups of homemade chicken stock, 1 finely chopped onion, and ¼ cup of chopped celery. Add salt and pepper to taste. Simmer and stir on medium-low heat for 20 minutes. Before serving, stir in one beaten egg and 3 teaspoons of sweet wine.

Small Acts

The broom understands receptivity. Receptivity is not passivity. Receptivity is the waiting, the synthesizing of the debris swept by the broom. It is at times bearing witness — watching the grass grow — knowing when to be receptive — being. It certainly is not "doing" a chore.

Sweep in your house, or community areas - take your broom as a flag of action to clean up the mess we left for future generations.

The art of divinization are the unmitagating endless small acts such as the act of sweeping which explores the unknown in observing cause and effect. The supposedly simple act of sweeping covers time and space concept, a space in which we live and need to know who we are, where we originated and to see the journey and migrations ahead of us. The broom clears the path before us in the art of divinization.

Mother Nature through the World Tree gave us a compass - the broom - for our journey. Examine the feelings you have when sweeping (not vacuuming). Is it resentment, slavery, or feeling under-appreciated? Who shares in the domestic tasks in your household — if anyone does? What does that say to you? If world government leaders and military men had to sweep up after themselves, would we have the violence we have had in our world for thousands of years?

Roast chestnuts in the embers of a hot fire during the late autumn and winter seasons. When roasting, sing a chant of your own pleas and words three times to honor the abundance given to you.

Evolutionary Memory: Envisioning the Future through the Kolo

Bird Goddess
Evolutionary Memory

Kolo Avenue: FOUR

Motif

E.C.M.
Integration of the past is paired with the future through memories. The future is manifested through intergenerational memory as seen in the dancing of the kolo when we share and are present in the circle.

The Bird Goddess reminds us of our South Slavic heritage through her role in oral tradition. These mentifacts (oral folklore) express kinship bonds and relationships with Baba Yaga, or Mother Nature.

*I*f memory is held sacred would we have intergenerational trauma or violence?

Sign

Research

The famous South Slavic wizard of electricity, Nikola Tesla, was able to memorize ample data, articles, and text as he orchestrated electricity for usage.[5] Tesla tapped his South Slavic heritage with mentifacts (oral folklore) as he expressed his kinship bonds and relations with Baba Yaga, also known as Mother Nature. Through memorization, Tesla was able to manifest the future with electricity; this is an example of evolutionary memory.

Storied Instructions

Victims of trauma respond with steel-reinforced denial. This denial swathed in steel means that Srebrenica war widows and their families have waited for many years for the return of their sons, brothers, husbands, and uncles, telling themselves that the men are only missing. Denial means not speaking of the reality, let alone facing it. I asked the Kolo Sumejja women and Srebrenica war widows why there were 100 years of war in their backyards and homes. The women responded in waves of blame that attest to the hierarchal property of our language and communications today, saying: "They came and took our sons, husbands, and uncles away."

Bioculinary

The elder tree, a hardwood, signifies Samhain, the thirteenth month. The *gulsa,* a South Slavic one-string guitar, is made from elder wood. *Dimnjaca,* or fumitory, is symbolized as smoky, rising flowers that are self-seeding. The flowers are used for making yellow dye and spread rapidly in ditches or magnificent fields.

The term *sahlep* refers to both the powder made from grinding dried tubers of the eastern European mountain orchid and the drink made with the powder. It is of Turkish and Jewish origins and flourished in Egyptian cuisine, showing its ancient connection to Orchis mascula, sold as a white powder in specialty stores. In Arabic, *sahlep* means "fox testicles" and correlates to the Greek work for orchid, which also carries an etymological association with testicles because of its shape. Though this now carries an aphrodisiacal or erotic connotation, its original, Stone Age purpose was to indicate that all sentient beings, humans and animals, belong to one family.

Sahlep is a traditional Turkish hot toddy drink known to heal sore throats and congestion. It can be thickened with steaming milk and seasoned with a bit of cinnamon and ginger; many have been known to place a scoop of homemade vanilla ice cream in the drink. In Sarajevo, the juice from the juniper berry is part of local tradition, for which the local coffeehouses are well-known. The century of war that has been perpetuated in part to retain control over the resources and ingredients necessary to perpetuate this tradition, however, goes largely unrecognized.

Sahlep

16 ounces of artesian well water and/or spring water
   (water not filtered by a water treatment plant)

2 tablespoons sahlep

6 ounces raw sugar

1 tablespoon cinnamon

½ pound rose petals

32 ounces water

2 lemons studded with cloves

Put *sahlep* powder into a small portion of water to moisten. Bring water and sugar to boil. Add in *sahlep* powder and you have the aphrodisiac drink.

To make rose juice, as is traditional in Bosnia, make sure the rose petals are cleaned and put in a large jar with cold water and the lemon-studded cloves. Put the jar on a shelf that gets the most sun exposure; as with making sun tea, let the rose petals meld into the water and lemon mixture until the petals are blanched white. Strain the water into a bowl and add in sugar, stirring with wooden spoons only. Pour into containers; it can be stored for nine days.

Small Acts

Donate funds or purchase a Kilim from Bosnia, Tuzla Srebrenica widows.
http://advocacynet.org/wordpress-mu/lzulkaphil/tag/hasan-nuhanovic/

The Cloud Woman: Air, Clouds, Rain, and the Goddess Dodola

Cloud Woman

Kolo Avenue: FOUR

Motif

E.C.M.
Rain and water are the first implements of ritual purification and remind us that death is always accompanied by life.

In the kolo, or round dance, young maidens dressed as trees chant rain songs, sparking the ages-old belief that we are walking trees and share a sister-kinship with the forests. Baba Yaga (Slavic Mother Nature) is, also, known as Cloud Woman.

*R*ecognizing the subtle phenomena of the female wisdom and wealth of life experiences passed down from the first mother wisdom in survivors' "right actions"

Sign

Research

Only Bulgarian Slavs and Serbians hold the ancient ritual called *Dodole* or *Perperuna* festivals when there is a drought. In a round kolo dance, young maidens dressed as trees chant rain songs, sparking the ages-old belief that we are walking trees and share a sister kinship with the forests and trees. It is only through the chanting of young women in their rich, green costumes resembling the trees in the kolo[6] that the Goddess Dodola is convinced to release the rain from the clouds.

Storied Instructions

Recognizing the subtle phenomena of the female wisdom and wealth of life experiences passed down from the first mother builds in survivors "right actions," such as reaching into the Moist Mother Earth for elements like water. For the South Slavic females who have survived wars and war crimes, moving from surviving to thriving requires a conscious attunement to the already established unconscious act such as that observed in the pattern of hiding in frigid waters as my paternal aunt, twin to my father, did in WWII with her three children. Many stories from the Balkan War repeated the same pattern of fleeing into the frigid waters in the former Yugoslavia.

Bioculinary

To make South Slavic coffee, you will need one and one half demitasse cups of boiling water, one heaping teaspoon of extra fine ground coffee, and one teaspoon of sugar.

The traditional way to make South Slavic coffee is in a *jesva*, or funnel-topped pot found in European, Arabic, or Turkish stores. Place water in a brass, silver, or copper *jesva*. Add sugar to one and one half demitasse cups of water. Let the water and sugar come to a roiling boil. Remove from heat and add coffee. Let the coffee foam to the top of the funnel and quickly remove from heat. Repeat this three times to ensure good coffee and to encourage good moisture to enrich your otherwise parched life. Holding the *jesva* high over the cup, pour the coffee; bring the *jesva* down as you pour so that a light, foamy frost forms. Serve. Do not stir or add cream.

Small Acts

Have a Blood and Honey dinner and coffee for your friends, neighborhood and/or communities.

Serve Bosnian (Arabic, Iranian, Serbian, Sudanese, Turkish, etc.) coffee. Read the grounds and share interpretations.

Letters of the Trees: Madrigals, or Singing Tree Rings

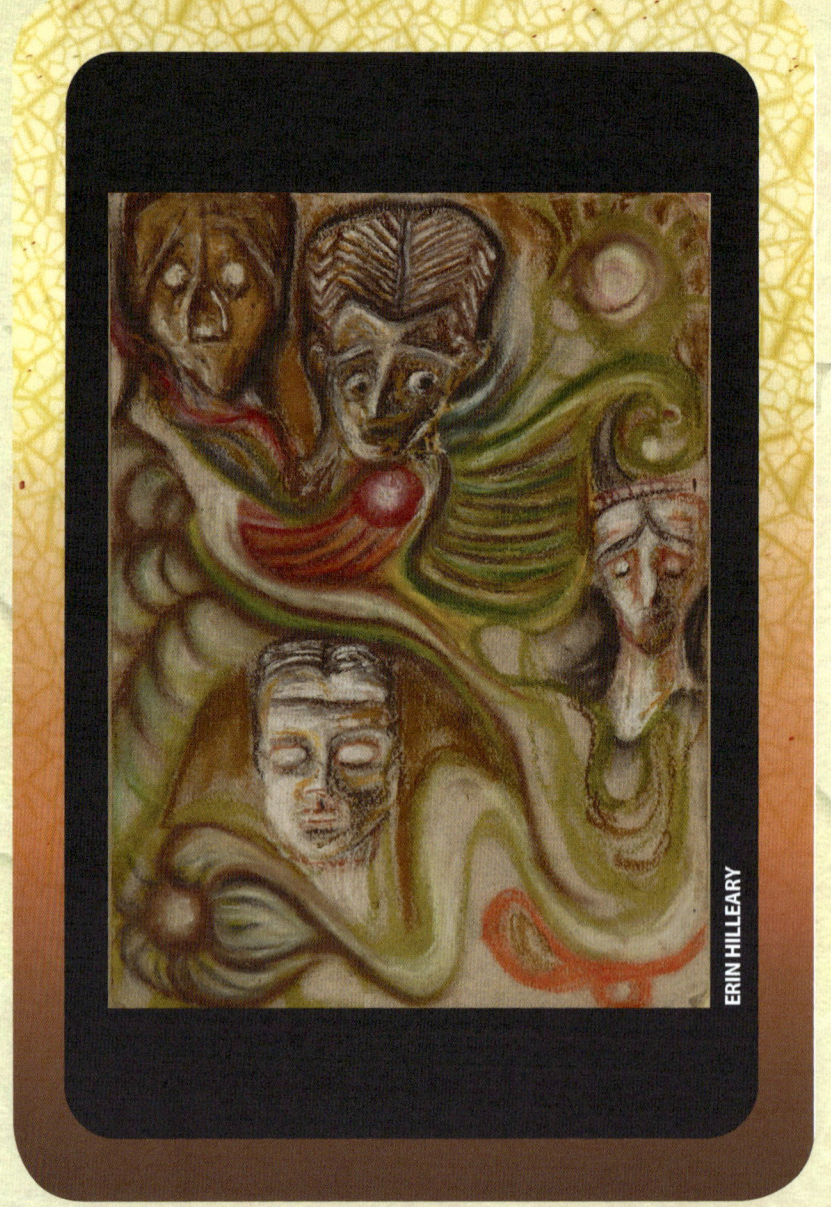

ERIN HILLEARY

Letters of the Trees

Kolo Avenue: FOUR

Motif

E.C.M.
The importance of the kolo as the umbilicus of community

*T*he word madrigal originally meant "a simple song from the mother's womb." Its root has come also to mean "to matriculate or to put on a list." The Latin noun "list" is derived from mater, or mother, and the Italian madrigale means "a simple unaccompanied song."

Sign

Research

The word madrigal originally meant "a simple song from the mother's womb."[7] Its root has come also to mean "to matriculate or to put on a list." The Latin noun "list" is derived from *mater*, or mother, and the Italian *madrigale* means "a simple unaccompanied song."

Storied Instructions

The Bosnian women war survivors and war crimes survivors, at various points in their lives, break out into the oldest chants taught to them by their mothers and grandmothers. Riding the crowded bus, working in the fields, fashioning their natural handmade brooms, or attending to the young, they sing their madrigals as they clean up after the war.

Bioculinary

Colewort, or *zecja stopa,* is a cabbage that does not form a head. It is used as a refrigerant, diuretic, and a cooling drink in febrile disorders. Colewort made into a salve stops itching.

Cheese Presnica

4 organic eggs, beaten

8 ounces natural organic brick cheese, broken into small pieces

¼ teaspoon salt

2 pounds organic small curd creamed cottage cheese

½ cup organic flour

¼ cup organic butter

½ cup organic milk

Melt butter. Brush a 13x9-inch glass pan with some of the melted butter. Combine the remaining ingredients except the butter in a mixing bowl. Pour into the glass pan. Drizzle remaining butter over the top of mixture. Bake at 350 degrees for one hour. Remove from oven and cool in pan.

Small Acts

1. How has your rhythm been disrupted and interrupted?
2. What unsung feminine madrigals exist within you that can heal the catastrophic violence and readdress the imbalance for the Moist Mother Earth?
3. When on your migrations (transitions in life and actual sacred pilgrimages) do you find fertile fields and fresh water to support you on your life's path?
4. Can you unravel the inherent wisdom within and passed down from mother to daughter for thousands and thousands of generations?

Responses to question one indicate initiation into painful consciousness about the reality of a woman's life experiences.

Responses to question two ask for responsibility of your life and the reality of your life experiences.

Responses to question three connect the ecology, the social dynamics in the virulent global violence towards females, minorities and children, and your own personal actions.

Responses to four reveal secret herstory of the greatest untold story of the mother and daughter bond.

Whirlpools and Spirals: Bird and Fish Goddess

Whirlpools and Spirals

Kolo Avenue: FOUR

Motif

E.C.M.
Life/Death/Life spiral
of regenerative potentials

Morava, the Mother of the Dead and the regenerative aspect of the Goddess, appears in four-to-six-thousand-year-old artifacts of the Bird and Fish Goddess that were found at Lepenski Vir.

*A*re you so desperate to dive to your death?

Sign

Research

Lepenski Vir, with its many caves, was used a temple and ritual work site on the Danube River, which is known for its whirlpools. The site is six-thousand-years-old and now faces a watery demise because of the building of a dam nearby in Serbia. Icons of the Serbian Mother of the Dead (Regenerative) Goddess Morava and the South Slavic Bird and Fish Goddess were found at Lepenski Vir that are estimated to be four to six thousand-years-old. Caves are also found in the Germanic matriarchal inheritance as *Frau Holla* (*Holle, Hell, Holda,* and *Perchta* through the ages). Frau *Holla-Hell,* or *Höhle,* is the German name for cave. The darkness of the cave is symbolized in South Slavic Bread, the braided bread made at the winter solstice. *Frau Holla* is also known as a rain and snow maker, a regenerator of Nature.

Storied Instructions

The Neretva River snakes below the newly reconstructed bridge now loaded with many German and Dutch tourists. While standing up on the thick stone rail, a diver taunts the crowd, "50 Euros to see me dive."

I asked the young man, "Are you so desperate to dive to your death for money?" He smiled at me. One of the Kolo Sumejja women on the bridge told me that young men there don't have a life. Another Kolo Sumejja woman demanded to know where his mother was. I had to laugh at that response, as the young man was at least twenty-five-years-old.

Bioculinary

The *holunder,* or elder tree, was the sacred tree of the Goddess, where her healing powers resided and where the dead lived. The following recipe is for braided egg bread and mineral water.

Serbian sweet braided egg bread has hard-cooked eggs dyed red resting on top of the braid. Red symbolizes the Lepenski Vir River of life, giving blood and death regenerative endowments. The Stone Age Fish Goddess (Regenerative) precept and recipe are carried on within the Serbian Orthodox religion, where red still represents the blood of Christ, and the eggs are a universal symbol of Christ's resurrection. Serbian Orthodox devotees also shape the dough into a cross with the red-dyed egg at the intersection. The Stone Age cross iconizes the crossing of truncated trees, the intersection of life and death. This recipe's symbolic representations in modern life show the double binding of two religions mixed into current father sky god religious cults.

For this recipe, use all organic materials, preferably home-grown or from within 50 miles of your residence.

Serbian Sweet Braided Egg Bread

- ½ cup cream
- ½ stick butter
- 1½ teaspoons vanilla, Zest of 1 lemon
- 2 teaspoons plus 2/3 cup sugar
- 1 package active dry yeast
- ¼ cup very warm water
- ¾ teaspoon salt
- ½ cup flour plus additional for dusting and shaping
- 5 large egg yolks & 2 whole large eggs
  Mineral Water
- 5 hard-cooked eggs, dyed red

Place heat cream, vanilla, and butter in a small saucepan on low heat. Melt butter. Dissolve sugar and yeast in warm water for 15 minutes. Add flour, salt, 2/3 cup sugar, and lemon zest. Add egg yolks, 1 whole egg, then cream and yeast mixture. Mix well until dough is sticky to the touch. Knead until smooth (dough is elastic), and add more flour as needed while kneading by hand. Grease bowl and place dough in it, coating dough with the oil. Let rise until double in size. Once risen, punch dough down and then divide into three portions. Shape each piece into a rope. Line the baking sheet with parchment, braiding the pieces. Take the red-dyed egg and place on dough so as to create a cradle. Pre-heat oven to 350 and cover the bread with a towel. Let rise for no more than twenty minutes. Beat remaining whole egg and brush top of braid.

Once out of the oven, sprinkle with mineral water, chanting wisdom and enlightenment. Serve with ghee (clarified butter) and homemade jam.

Small Acts

The journey from Novi Travnik along the Neretva River has me focused upon the insight that healing starts within each individual when fully felt emotional and feeling experience is involved. The reciprocal side of this insight means, that each individual's small acts and actions are a co-created process that ripples across the globe.

Archeoquests
- How does the river of time bend back on itself in your life? For instance, do you catch yourself saying, "I should have done…" or "If I could have seen or known that…" throughout your life with significant events. The South Slavic ancient grandmothers in their reverence of Lepenski Vir, the whirlpools of time where they honored the deaths of their children, eloquently appeared to know that such bending back in time causes bitterness and control issues (another face of fear). Surrendering into Baba Yaga/Mother Nature's arms where so-called 'negative' events actually induce one to transverse the river of time dropping any notion of earlier or later. 'Earlier' is the sense of time that is found in linguistic usage of the word 'when' and indicates

impulsive and compulsive approaches. 'Later' sense of time is found in the word usage of 'never' populating procrastinations, judgments and harsh criticisms. When dropping the constrictive and bending back the river of time earlier or later as indicators for time we repel the bitterness and control issues. We learn from mistakes and trauma is that intensified learning engagement and environment that moves us through and evolves us.

- Have you ever felt like the world is spinning after a catastrophic event? Mother Nature/Baba Yaga parallels the spinning with her whirlpools and spinning Moist Mother Earth bringing in an inward force you never realized until the catastrophic event. What inward forces can you recognize? Merging positive and negative energy after catastrophic or negative events incurs the wrath of Baba Yaga/Mother Nature where it is impossible to manipulate and deny your way out of the extremely difficult state. In fact like the whirlpool and spiral eddies an individual is sucked down beyond any human control. For positive and negative energies to coexist, authenticity and being in your feelings stabilizes the spinning. You become the weaver or the time traveler that does not violate Mother Nature's laws.

Invisibility and Transparency

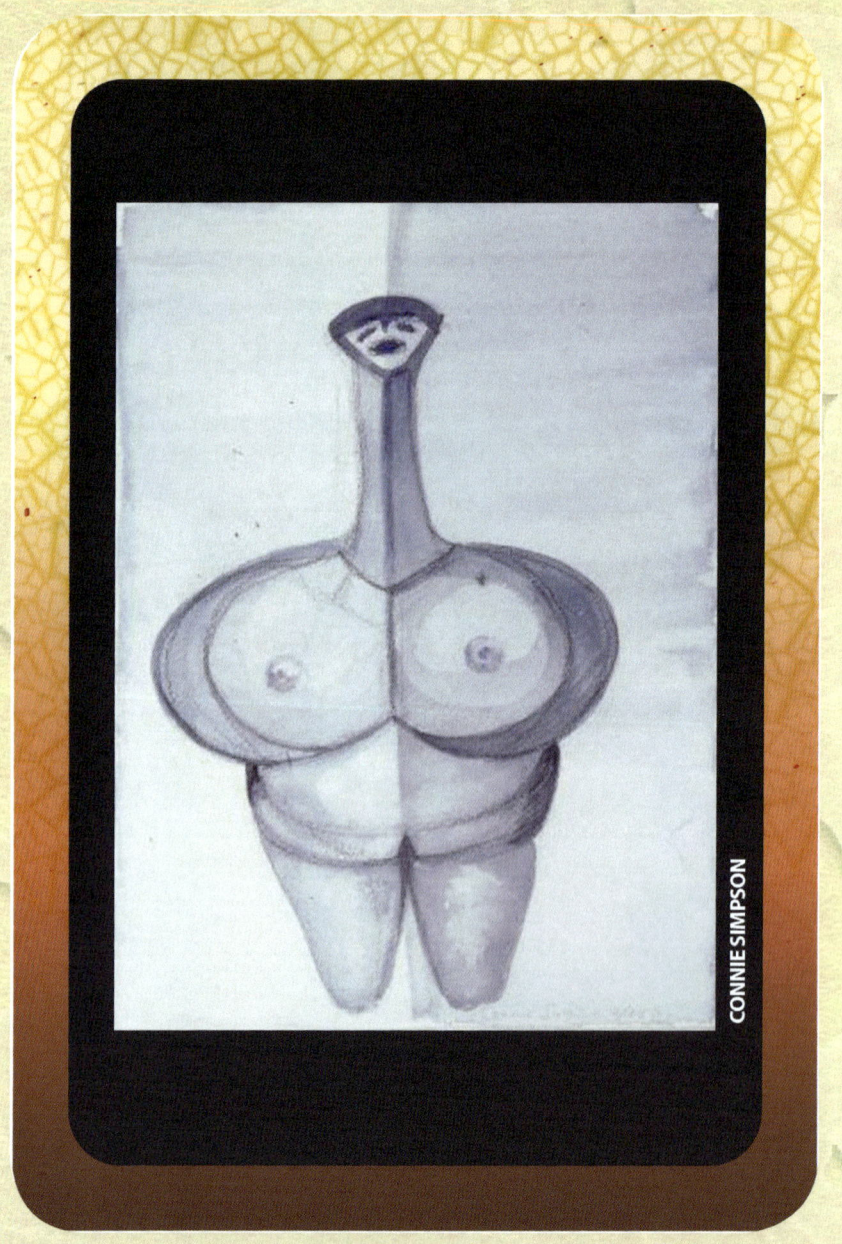

CONNIE SIMPSON

Invisibility & Transparency

Kolo Avenue: THREE

Motif

E.C.M.
Truth is transparent, invisibility is made transparent.

The greater the asymmetry, the greater the effect on the velocity. The latter describes the pull toward the invisible first person stories of the South Slavic peoples and all peoples.

*T*he scope of what was transparent reflected the pairing of beauty with ugliness.

Sign

Research

Visible within the ancient artifacts found in the former Yugoslav lands is a lived practice being performed by the South Slavs. Despite being pounded by catastrophic wars and rapes, South Slavs still manifest what is invisible, and I was able to witness and be moved by it. What were the spaces or places that can be felt with invisibility and transparency? A prime example is the velocity of satellites Pioneer 10 & 11, set on a course to move out of our solar system. According to scientists, they are acting on essentially unknown laws of Mother Nature: the greater the asymmetry, the greater the effect on the velocity. The latter describes the pull towards the invisible first-person stories of South Slavic peoples.

Storied Instructions

The polar opposites glared at me as I took in the Bosnian landscape. The scope of what was transparent reflected the pairing of beauty with ugliness. Full, sylvan mountainsides paired with stewing garbage hit my senses. Two things struck me as particularly poignant; a hot, fragrant, delicious meal selected from the garbage and cooked by Roma hands in a rubber tire and an exquisite, doll-like Roma female infant born on a mountainside where refuse is pitched.

Bioculinary

In Russia, kasha is made from buckwheat flour. Kasha is associated with Slavic burials and weddings—rebirth and birth—and is prepared for holidays such as Whitsun, the Winter Solstice, housewarming parties, and sowing and reaping rituals. This recipe is for South Slavic liqueur.

Kasha

South Slavic liqueur was used as a medicinal practice for cold and insomnia ailments. As with all bioculinary recipes, organic materials, especially those grown by your own hand, are preferred.

The peels of 24 oranges

2 pounds cubed sugar

1 Quart Slivovica (Serbian Plum Brandy)

All the ingredients are placed into a covered gallon jar. Shake thoroughly every morning for anywhere from thirty to forty days. Using a cheesecloth, strain and pour into glass bottles.

Small Acts

Braiding Truth/Essentials (Plasma) with Insights

Three pieces of paper are needed and a pen to write the following:

- Think of what is true for you and essential right now in your life.
- List when you shape shifted into transparency (the powerful moments of insights-Aha!)?
- Now Weave together the stories of what is your truth and essential with examples of transparency

Ask

1. What has rhythm to it?
2. What was laborious spadework in the past? The tremendous amount of small acts that built your life or passion is the spadework I write of. Raising a child is laborious spadework, writing a book, or article.
3. Which events or situations in your life had intense cleansing followed by breakthrough?

The recipe for shape shifting into transparency begins with what we value and how often we "be" in that value. These are often called "beliefs" but note that the word "belief" has the word, "lie" in it. Truth is an outcome of value and becomes plasma. With values lived and applied with truth ever present in our moments, we will shape shift immediately.

Small Acts

Hide and Seek

Play the game of hide and seek in the forest with another person. Instruct one person to hide alongside the forest path. The others will wait for a period of time before walking the same path to seek their hiding place. As they walk the path to see the unseen/invisible whenever they sense the hiding person's energy, they will call out their name—manifesting transparency/becoming visible to you.

The person who is hiding practices the skill of being invisible—at one with the trees, the land and the birds. To feel one's connection with the hiding place accepts the truth that we are all one family and becomes one with all our relations.

With Hide and Seek, we see the depth and span of invisibility and transparency. To seek is to be authentic (invisible), in your own truth. To seek authenticity and truth is enlightenment becoming transparent to all sentient beings.

The Seekers in the game of hide and seek practice in remembering their psychic/ physics reading skills—a precursor to silent reading done in our modern era. The Hide-n-Seek players can sense the many paths taken towards concealment by the one hiding and becoming invisible. At the end of the game, both the parties are astounded at how accurate the seeker was in tracing the players' paths towards the hiding places.

We learn and remember our ability to be invisible when we need to. The Hide-n Seek game highlights transparency. For instance note how transparency occurs when there is a need of energy and harmony in life. Transparency is plasma birthed from our feelings, authenticity and truth.

Guardian Dogs

Guardians- Dogs

Kolo Avenue: FOUR

Motif

E.C.M.
Witness bearers much like the ancient trees in recording the earth-wide migrations and seasons of earth, humans, and other species

Dog phylogeny is a science that hopes to trace the crossbreeding and back breeding that has occurred through millions of years. When we peer into a dog's origins, we are peering at the first human mother and seeing her great powers of observation and wisdom through her careful animal husbandry.

*C*anis Familiaris Matris Optimale appears to be the only dog revered by the South Slavs, regardless of what their religion dictates.

Sign

Research

Of the four subspecies of the family dog dating back at least 10,000 years, the Bosnian *Tornjak* is traced to *Canis Familiaris matris- Optimale*. This is a dingo or pariah-like dog (associated with a sheepdog function) found in the Mt. Carmel caves and in Persia, where it is descended from the Arab and South Asian Wolves.

Another association, or ancient migratory memory, occurs with South Slavs who breed the *Tornjak* seeking an all-white coat. This is comparable to the American Eskimo dog or the white dogs called *Bjelkiers* from the far northern tribes.

Storied Instructions

Thousands of dogs were left on the streets during and after the Balkan war, many of their owners dead or too poor to feed their faithful companions. I was haunted by the pack of dogs occupying the site of a destroyed apartment building; generations of dogs waited for their original owners to come back, but no one ever would return. Packs of dogs roam the streets and countryside tearing each other up, leaving ear bits and dog body parts after a harsh night of warring on the already stained Bosnian streets.

Bioculinary

Cukvarkuca, or common mountain house leek, grows in the Bosnian mountains and Dinaric Alps. The plant has hermaphroditic (male and female) flowers. The leaves are used in salads and for purposes similar to the aloe plant. The plant stretches across the Southeastern mountains into Iran, depicting the migration of the *Tornjak*.

Sana Koric would take me to the fields where the best nettle grew. I asked her why she did not grow her own, and she told me that the nettle is best if grown wild and on its own. Gatherers select only the most succulent, and the Slavs believe that the wildness of the plant adds to its nutritional value. During the Balkan Wars, nettles saved many from starvation.

Nettle Pirjan

1 pound Nettle leaves

3 pounds lamb

1 cup wild rice soaked overnight in artesian waters

Tablespoon red pepper and salt and ground white pepper

Tablespoon of ghee

Chop the nettle leaves and place in a pot. Place lamb seasoned with salt and ground pepper in roasting dish with a cup of water. Roast in oven at 425 degrees, and when cooked, take ½ cup of water from roasting pan and add to the nettles. Bring nettles to boil and add wild rice and ghee. Add water as needed for the wild rice. Season with red pepper, ground white pepper, and salt.

Small Acts

According to South Slavs, Baba Yaga/Moist Mother Earth always has the last word.

- Have you volunteered to train dogs for those in need and whose migratory paths in life are with great challenges and exalted duties for the rest of us to be inspired by?
- If you have dogs and pets, are they neutered and taken care of in small acts such as feeding, watering, walking daily and so on? What stories or memories of pets are handed down as a part of the family album?
- In third world countries or war torn countries like Bosnia, dogs are neglected, abused, tortured, and at times they run in packs. Donating funds, time and services to help stem this problem would be a magnified small act.

Pech (Round Beehive Stove)

Pech- Round Beehive Stove

Motif

E.C.M.
The fire – the light heals everything and restores essential form from which to seed new life.

Kolo Avenue: TWO

In archaeological findings, the bread oven usually had benches around it where some of the earliest artifacts in European history were found (6,300 to 6,100 BCE).

Now, tragically reduced to a mere few incandescent appeals for mercy and remembrance for those ethically cleansed.

Sign

Research

The Vinlovic-Samogyvdr culture at Trznica, Srem, in northern former Yugoslavia (25th-21st centuries BCE) shows the layering of ancient female uteri wisdom emerging through Kurgan (the Father Sky God cult). A Kurgan patriarchal hierarchy from late in the period of Yamna culture in what is now known as the former Yugoslavia reflected the South Slavic peoples' culture.[8] Stone lime pits with four posts and sometimes roofed structures were built for the South Slavic *stari Babas* (Serbo-Croatian for wise woman or grandmother) who practiced cremation with their fiery *pechs*.

Storied Instructions

Three iconic references to the *pech* presented themselves to me in the immeasurably frigid air found in Novi Travnik, Bosnia. One was the *pech* mutated into metal garbage containers, another the remaining few brave lights from the mountain village Lazine, and the third the fact that the day I visited was *Imbolc,* or Candlemas, and the Croatian Catholic Day of Bread celebration. On February 2, 2003, in very cold mountain air with a crystal snowscape in the town, I walked home to Sana Koric's house after a kolo meeting. Along the way, Sana pointed to the mountain side to show me a village that had a few lights.

This village, which was once full of many lights, reminded me of how the women and their families had rebelled and returned home despite waiting for permission from the U.N. for years. This formerly thriving village was now tragically reduced to a mere few incandescent appeals for mercy and remembrance for those ethnically cleansed. As I glanced up to the mountain on the cold, small street, a garbage container combusted and shot up with hot flames.

Bioculinary

The *Smilje*, or curry plant, is an ancient reminder of when forests were transforming into steppes. It is particularly aromatic on a hot day in late afternoon.

> This recipe is for *pogacha*, which is quick or flat bread best baked in the beehive ovens that prevail throughout former Yugoslavia. Bosnian women spoke of having no electricity, only their *pechs* for baking this bread.

Pogacha

- 2 packages of dry yeast
- 2 teaspoons salt
- ½ cup water
- 2 tablespoons honey/sugar
- 4 to 5 cups plus 2 tablespoons organic flour
- 1/3 cup yellow coarse ground cornmeal-organic
- 1-1/2 cups warm water
- ¼ cup oil

Empty in a bowl the 2 packages of yeast, ½ cup of warm water, and 2 tablespoons flour. Stir. Put in a warm place, such as the oven or hearth, to rise. Combine the 1½ cups water and remaining ingredients and add raised yeast mixture. Gradually add flour and mix. Knead lightly until the dough is soft and very smooth. Divide in two and let the dough rest for nine minutes. Press down and shape the smooth dough (which represents fetal material) into a 9-inch round pan. Sprinkle the cornmeal (say a blessing or chant when doing so) on a flat cookie sheet and place the two dough halves onto the cornmeal. Let rise until doubled in size. Bake at 375 for 30-45 minutes.

Small Acts

Summer Kuchen- Summer Kitchens in former Yugoslavia- Bosnia was often placed near the garden avaluas. Avluas are gazebos or fully enclosed structures that often have roses or vines with plentiful flowers. Known as Mutvak, the summer kitchen was often connected to the house or close to the house. Winter Kuchen-Winter Kitchens are in the main hearth in the home/domovi. In any similar areas of your home of artisan coffee house do the following:

- Notice how fire melts into other fires with raging speed. Fire burns away the past and allows us to mourn our losses—so we can be in this exact moment. Carefully burn a log or other materials with permits if required in areas most like the Avluas such as camp fires, or control fires permitted at home.

- Do you enjoy a mother/daughter-son relationship which ignites honor, growth, transformation and pain (pain is a storied instruction saying we are alive and present) into your spiritual being? Do a remembrance mantra each morning: I am born of woman: every single person regardless of gender was born of a woman.

- Place pictures of loved ones, angel/bird/witch figures in the kitchen, gleaming pots to represent the Mistress of the Hearth near your stove. When we (both genders) are in pregnancy, whether physically or in our art making-creativity, the feminine spirituality within us is purified in the flames and rises from the ashes with the clarity of ceramic boldness and depth.

BLOOD & HONEY

Tree Rings

Tree Rings

Motif

E.C.M.
Slavic Ethnogenesis –
Cellular Memory – Civilization –
Memories

Kolo Avenue: THREE

Roots are considered magical in South Slavic folklore, and South Slavs still train ash tree branches into a Y-shaped intersection.

"*I*ma trava u okolo Save, I korenja okolo jasenja" translates into "There are herbs by the Sava [River in Serbia], and roots around ash trees." [1]

Sign

Research

The letters of the trees and tree rings indicate South Slavic female humanity and culture where a concentric and cyclical pattern is symbolized and conjured in the present moment in the female realms of the conjugal home, in her womb, and in the very tree rings. Both the womb and tree rings represent cellular memory in mitochondrial DNA and in the tree ring record. The Slavic language still refers to the "letters" of the trees. The kolos "list" and "letter" our humanity within Mother Earth, expressed through embodied dance steps or being in a spiraling circle dance—kolo— shoulder-to-shoulder with others. Classically trained archeologist Marija Gimbutas traced the cradle of Proto-Slavic spiral art and determined that Slavic plant terminology for the deciduous trees located in the forest steppe and steppe belt are "in agreement with archeological reconstructions of the environment of prehistoric Slavic culture."[9]

Storied Instructions

The kolo is the circle of life for South Slavs. This was not so for an elderly grandmother who lived in Novi Travnik, Bosnia. On the outskirts of town, she was standing deep in thought next to a sunny wall. Her black and red *babushka* was tied tightly and she held a handkerchief in her hand.

I startled her with my greeting. She waved her handkerchief to tell me to come to her.

No introductions or names passed our lips, since she started talking immediately as if she had been waiting for me all her life. Citing loneliness as an illness that made her terminal breast cancer seem insignificant, she dabbed her tear-filled eyes. Speaking as if her life depended on it, she said the kolo and all it represents had been missing from her life, her mother's life, and her grandmother's life because of three wars.

She mentioned the Bird Flu epidemic of 1918 as well, as if the trauma of so much death was the culprit that erased the kolo round dances. The ritual kolo round dances did not impose control or tell anyone the meaning of life; rather, she thought the kolo encouraged each dancer to share her first person story as we search for our own meanings.

Bioculinary

Jasika - Aspen tree not the Slavic world tree which has the oak tree as it representative, folk veterinary medicine.

Of course, organic or grown within 150 miles of your home or pech (stove) stands for every Bioculinary recipe. The Birds' Nests are another iconic Bird Goddess form, like the bread molded in likeness of the tree, representing the circle of connection and relations of the cosmos. Imagine the difference in the taste in growing your own nut tree, your home made jam from your own fruit trees on your property or close by.

Pticija Gnjezda - Birds Nests

1 cup of butter   2 egg whites

½ brown sugar   2 cups ground nuts

2 egg yolks   2 tablespoons powdered sugar

2 cups sifted flour   jelly for filling

Put butter and sugar into a bowl and cream. Add in the egg yolks and beat. Add flour and mix until smooth. Roll into small balls and then beat the egg whites with a fork until foamy.

Dip balls into egg whites and in 2 cups of ground nuts mixed with 2 tablespoons powdered sugar. Place on cookie sheet and press centers with thimble. Bake at 325 degrees for 5 minutes-remove and press centers again. Bake for 10-13 minutes longer. Fill centers with jelly while warm.

Small Acts

Storied Instructions for the kolo begin with:

1. Join a folk dancing instructions group.
2. If you know the round dances- dance the kolos every six days if not more.

Other forms of the kolo dance if you are not up to the dance or postures immediately:

- Start to embroider cloth with your symbolic and significant meanings for growth, blossoming, birth, death-ripening, and harvest. Weave and embroider for 13 months while in a kolo/circles with at least one or many individuals.
- Make a dowry necklace- three loops that hang across the chest. Select charms, jewels or round coins to place on the strands.
- Go to the forest or to a tree, a picture whose posture calls to your soul. Can you mirror the posture for three minutes in silence?
- Walk, stand or sit regally with full female glory at least 13 times throughout your day/night when you can. This creates horizontal and vertical sacred space immediately.

144

Ψ BLOOD & HONEY Ψ

Bird Goddess Wings & Claws

CONNIE SIMPSON

Bird Goddess
Evolutionary Memory

Kolo Avenue: FOUR

Motif

E.C.M.
Integration of the past is paired with the future through memories. The future is manifested through intergenerational memory as seen in the dancing of the kolo when we share and are present in the circle.

The Bird Goddess reminds us of our South Slavic heritage through her role in oral tradition. These mentifacts (oral folklore) express kinship bonds and relationships with Baba Yaga, or Mother Nature.

*I*f memory is held sacred would we have intergenerational trauma or violence?

Sign

Research

In the past forty years alone, we have witnessed the doubling of international migrants; 175 million, or about 3.5 percent of the world's population, are transient, and half of these are women.[10] "Whether voluntarily or involuntarily, women have become a growing 'export' from many developing countries around the world."[11] The United Nations report by Ren Kukanesen says that the Bosnian female diaspora is being headed by elderly women with meager incomes, and that they are the main providers for displaced peoples and war-wounded individuals. The report discovered that, of the female-headed Bosnian households surveyed, ninety-eight percent of those women were widows.

The partnership of wings and claws portrays the Bird Goddess's aspect of the Family Rod Goddess with the face of the Fish and Snake Goddesses. Marija Gimbutas named this conglomeration the Goddesses of Death and Regeneration. Protectress of life, energy, and health, the Family Goddess (*Podrodica* in Serbo-Croatian) takes the zoomorphic forms of Bird and Snake. Goddesses gave way to birth-givers, nurses, and Madonnas, which are essentially all of one body and one family.

Storied Instructions

Many of the Bosnian women cloistered together during the siege reported their menses synchronizing, just like the sharing of a single spoon among many. Recalling female solidarity and female coalitions in times of crisis and war, one young woman remarked that she yearns for that circle-kolo now in the aftermath of war. She stated hostility and hatred combined in competition as women sought to survive after the war eradicated female solidarity. She asked, "Do I need to wish for another war to have that harmony with women again?"

Bioculinary

Ocajnica- White Horehound, ocarinjen in Serbo-Croatian means duty paid— used for coughs, clams a nervous heart, aids digestion and liver functions.

Dagara-crepulja-earthen dish of lamb

Make an earth dish with lid with your own hands.

Do this dish during the waxing period and full moon only. Grow home-grown or local yellow onions diced.

Grow 3 stalks of celery diced.

Grow garlic to use an entire garlic clove- sliced-grated and left in clarified butter

(ghee) with paprika and salt

Grow 6 Home grown tomatoes

Grow red potatoes 7-13 red potatoes – medium size not small- sliced

3 lbs of lamb & 3 lbs beef without bones- organic and local cut into serving pieces

8 ounces water-artesian well or spring—no water treatment plant or water stored in plastic bottles.

With clean fingers, spread ghee in the crepulja. Layer first meat, then the vegetables and end with potatoes as top layer. Add the 8 ounces of water, and clover crepulja bake in oven 425 for 40 minutes and reduce to 325 for another 45 minutes.

Small Acts

There is a chant—women's song—that speaks of being born from the Birch tree:

Tu ima devet imade sestrica—who has nine sisters?

I pred njma Vila nastarya—eldest in front

We are molded and shape shifted by the environment and the interactions with the Moist Mother Earth. Scientists are just now scratching at the surface of what Baba Yaga-Mother Nature has encoded in DNA blueprints which are "an accumulation of over three billion years of evolution." John Liption, *Biology of Belief,* (Mountain of Love/Elite Books, 2005) p. 86

Your quest is to plan an hour's worth of expression—your beliefs, values and wisdom you have lived. Reflect on how your grandmothers died—was it with grace and dignity? Who was there to witness their deaths and listen for an hour? Who is your nine sisters? Who is your eldest sister?

Creatively design a collective archive of the truth unsaid (you have three billion years of evolution) to instigate a collective social movement or support a social movement.

Ψ BLOOD & HONEY Ψ

Yawning Bird Goddess

Yawning Bird Goddess Synchronization

Motif

Kolo Avenue: THREE

E.C.M.
Signals a migratory cycle, a sacred pilgrimage, whether physical or spiritual. Symbolizes rhythm, synchronicity, and spontaneous collaboration among groups and circles of living things.

A non-conscious, or super-conscious, ability is yawning. Like menstrual cycles, yawns are often synchronized in close groups. Robert Svobda, a disciple of India Aghora (Great Mother Worship), remarked that "while all the animals yawn, even fish and reptiles, psychotics or the severely ill rarely do. Yawning is a sign that they are beginning to recover. Do not suppress yawning."

Ill and seemingly blind, she begged for death to come.

Sign

Research

The South Slavic *stara baba* knew that yawning and bleeding work together as steps of synchronization, a synchronicity that leads toward solidarity and is most likely based on their life experiences in raising children and growing food from the Moist Mother Earth. The South Slavs' intimate wisdom of the body's way of learning is what scientists call the mirror-neuron system.

"This circuitry is called the mirror-neuron system because it contains a special type of brain cells, or neurons, that become active both when their owner does something and when he or she senses someone else doing the same thing. Mirror neurons typically become active when a person consciously imitates an action of someone else, a process associated with learning."[12]

The Bird Goddess's deep, ecological embrace understood the contagious yawns as repeating and replicating behaviors that do not begin with left brain functions of reason or logic. Yawning as a practice strikes at the core of what is universal from the seat of being; the Bird Goddess of Rejuvenation symbolically represents the ability to have and to be a part of great movements such as the flight of migrations on equinoxes and the ability to have ovarian synchrony.

Storied Instructions

There is no way that I could distance myself from the stench, the last days of a grandmother without her daughter or grandchildren, or the stories from the Kolo Sumejja women. I realized that I would not want to and pushed myself up another flight of increasingly dark steps, hearing the scurrying feet of rats ahead. At first, when I saw the grandmother lying still on the couch, I thought she had already died. We sat down slowly, talked to her, and touched her shoulder. The grandmother awoke and became confused. Ill and seemingly blind, she begged for death to come. She was not confused, however; she was focused for flight, an immediate departure.

A Canadian gentleman found my website and related that his refugee friends' mother lived in Travnik, near Novi Travnik. He requested that I go visit the mother. The seeming randomness of his finding the Kolo: Women's Cross Cultural Collaboration was significant. There is a synchronized pattern evident through the need of the very ill Bosnian grandmother dying alone. We went to witness her last days.

Bioculinary Recipe

Gentiana lutea Gentian contains some of the most bitter substances known, particularly the glycosides gentiopicrin and amarogentin. The taste of these can be detected even when diluted 50,000 times. Besides stimulating secretion of saliva in the mouth and hydrochloric acid in the stomach, gentiopicrin may protect the liver, indigestion and poor appetite.

Ajvar- Eggplant & Pepper Relish

2 eggplants	6 green peppers	2 hot chili peppers
salt/pepper to taste	fresh lemon juice- 1 lemon	
parsley	1 cup oil	2 cloves garlic crushed

Bake eggplants and peppers in hot oven, 375 degrees for 30-45 minutes until tender—turn peppers occasionally to prevent blistering. Remove the skins, and any seeds while hot. Chop eggplants and peppers finely and place into a blender, add salt, pepper, crushed garlic with lemon juice and oil- blend.

Observe how the hot oven is the womb and life's challenges. The metaphor in turning the peppers remarks on the process of not being burned by our migratory patterns in life or flying too close to the sun with our egos. Removing the skins and seeds while hot reminds us to sort through our life and obstacles. Blending the ingredients combine the two kolo avenues, Avenue Three and Four. Spread the Ajvar on freshly made kolach/ bread.

Small Acts

When was the last time you experienced a great movement—a collective pool of consciousness—where it had meaningfulness and values that mirror your own without having to do it bureaucratically or in linear fashion (meaning without having to register to march, to look at legal steps, or to climb up the ladder doing fanatically hard work)?

Eternal memory is the place where a female's life experiences that evolutionize rather then revolutionize are a part of her DNA. What events in your life do you feel will be handed down through the next nine generations?

Write a poem. Go to a poetry reading, read other poems.

Watch people—are they present?

Are you in touch with the wonders of life daily?

What wonders are present in your life?

What if the large groups of people such as an airport had the V formation of birds- what would that look like?

Stare at the grandmothers' picture and envision what your last days would be. Reflect on how you want to die.

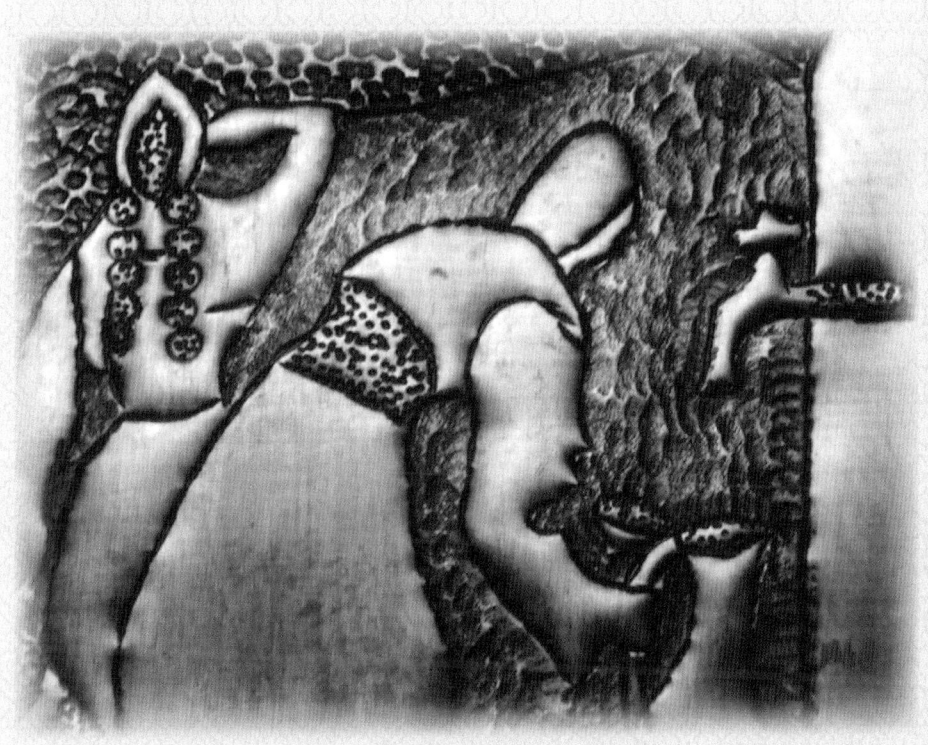

Bearing Witness, Transmigration, Metempsychosis, and Regeneration

ERIN HILLEARY

Bearing Witness

Kolo Avenue: FOUR

Motif

E.C.M.
Channel fecund material and life-giving wisdom into form with rituals and reverence born from bearing witness and appealing to Mother Earth.

Metempsychosis eyes are the concentric circles found in South Slavic archaeological sites and artifacts. Their impact ripples through the generations as we rediscover ancient Paleolithic and Neolithic ways of life.

Sign

Research

The kolo round dances or circles include needle work that reflects the metempsychosis transmigrations of Paleo/Neolithic vital life functions that have been reincarnated into the present moment. The vital life functions of females, such as menstrual synchrony and ethnography, are iconized in transmigrations through artifacts and into present material evidence. Transmigration is the sacred pilgrimage sometimes referred to as rebirth, or metempsychosis. Orphic doctrine refers to this shift through the symbology of a thunderbolt or meteoric stone.[13] Bearing witness and hearing first person stories are thunderbolts and meteoric stones thrown into your being and consciousness.

Storied Instructions

During the siege of Novi Travnik, snipers took up locations in the surrounding heavily treed hills. Going to the market meant a ten-second dash and spurts of diving for cover. Many were killed on their way to the market and even as they stayed hidden in their flats or homes away from windows; the snipers were still able to intrude into their homes. However, one young Bosnian woman was able to get out and make forays to the mountain slopes for herbs, plants, and berries. After the war, an elder woman from another village, who knew her great-grandmother, went to her. The elder woman told her how proud her great-grandmother would be that she followed in her footsteps and knew the plants, herbs, and mushrooms that would help feed her family.

The mysteries deepened when the young woman revealed that she had no idea of her great-grandmother's stored wisdom and had never before been interested in botany. She said that she simply felt guided to pick the mushrooms and plants. The transmigration of wisdom occurs in this fashion and is especially heightened during times of trauma when the need to survive is great.

Bioculinary

Planatin, Snakeweed plant is used to treat stomachaches and other internal disorders such as diarrhea. When chopped and mixed with clarified butter, it is a poultice for wounds.

Bioculinary Recipe:

White Halva- Desserts-sweets

12 ounces of hazelnuts

4 eggs ¼ cup sugar

13 tablespoons of honey

Use only the egg white and whip until peaks are formed. Add in the sugar and stir in until blended. Place in pan on low heat, the honey stirring constantly like a hummingbird. Add in the egg whites and sugar and turn off the flame. Chop up or crunch by hand the hazelnuts. Have wax paper or parchment paper on a plate and place the white Halva onto it—pressing down until it has spread evenly. Cut into twenty four pieces, remove paper before eating.

Small Acts

Transmigration is pilgrimage and sometimes referred to as rebirth, metempsychosis/ regeneration. This in Orphic doctrine is noted as the symbology of a thunderbolt or meteoric stone. (Robert Graves, *White Goddess*, p. 283) Bearing witness and hearing first person stories are thunderbolts and meteoric stones thrown into your being and consciousness.

From sacred observations, women can demand poetic justice and know solidarity with other women who also shared their first-person stories. The first-person stories across cultures are universal and known to all women.

By bearing witness solidarity threaded into our beings with other women, we discover how effortlessly it is to bear witness and that it was not a struggle.

Explore what activates curiosity and awe within you. Can you describe what gives you curiosity or awe?

Blood and Honey Icon Pedagogy Book Template

- Map of Cups = Blueprint of four categories replicating the learning process
- The Nest is the Kolo = Four Concentric Circles, Kolo = to dance the round dances or to be in the circle.
- Kolo Four Avenues = Spiraling Directions-Guidance, Memory Depth Work
- Archetypal Chapter Movements, Meta-Definitions = Blood and Honey Icons
- Bioculinary = Alchemical, Transformative Agency- Foraging, Agrarian practices, recipes
- Paleolithic Motifs = Natural organization and structure of ancestral memory
- South Slavic Female Symbology and Female Humanities = Intangible Heritage

What is Blood and Honey Pedagogy?

The teachings and narratives of Blood and Honey Icons are experiential and offer an immediate path to understanding. The book fosters bearing witness to oneself and others, which is healing. Biosemiotics celebrates the healers we always have been and will always be. Tangible learning approaches that work through multi-disciplinary fields intermixed with experiential venues, practicum, and mutual exchange best describe the Blood and Honey pedagogy and book template.

My learning style can be evidenced in both my in-depth research and the inspiring wisdom of the women I observed in the aftermath of catastrophic events. I studied the elements of the ancient South Slavic women's narrative that appeared in a modern world of catastrophic violence. This is the point at which traumatized peoples embrace crisis as a period of intensified learning and move from surviving to thriving. My immersion in the world of refugees and victims of violence provided me a perspective not found in reading lists or core curricula. Crisis and disaster protocol and responses for psychological import became evident through my study.

I explore female culture and it is a matrifocal trauma format based on the kolo. Archeological artifacts and scripts, from archeomythologies to Jungian archetypes and symbolism, were found to provide depth and breadth to my trauma research and actual trauma work in the field involving somatic psychology and neuroscience. I was able to apply the instructions and experiments in the book in Africa, Bosnia, India, and Sri Lanka, which demonstrates their universal relevance.

In exploring the Blood and Honey curriculum, the pedagogy, fostered through online coursework from my book materials and numerous workshops, led to break-through intensives at archeological sites throughout Europe in conjunction with Marija Gimbutas's work and unique workshops for students and interns. The Kolo: Womens' Cross Cultural Collaboration Non-Profit Organization provides apprenticeships as opposed to internships. Apprentices explore the potency found in past life experiences and their own life experiences.

My witnessing those surviving and still living in trauma has become an unrivalled university or Poetic College and a place where my research and continued work to learn, explore, and discover healing practices sparks awe and intense curiosity. The purpose of the Blood and Honey book template is to impart healing through awe and curiosity.

The template is what I have learned from my professors on the frontlines, many of whom lack even a kindergarten-level education. Certainly, my book and the pedagogical card deck I developed are intensified learning available to all who will embrace a full-bodied discourse about what I have witnessed, observed, and lived during the past decade with Bosnian women war survivors and war crimes survivors; the African women of Chad, Congo, Sudan, and Uganda; and women in India and Sri Lanka.

Readers can interface with the raw data that I have uncovered, allowing them to experience a mutual exchange with intergenerational trauma and both find and research ways to evolve through the wounds and scars of trauma. The Blood and Honey approach focuses on knowing what we do not know. We cannot know what we do not know if we lack the relevant life experiences. In other words, we cannot learn about the ancient past embedded in our minds and bodies without adding our own life experiences to the intergenerational communication that takes place through female social collective practices. Adding this to your life will help you expand a larger temporal stream in your own understanding.

What are the Kolo Avenues and the Map of Cups?

The circular form of the Slavic kolo dance is important and gives us information about both biosemiotics and the female social collective. The kolos are often repeated in various shapes, forms, and rhythms. Dendrology, the study of tree rings and the exquisite circular pattern of birds' nests, reveals the continuity in the seemingly random patterns found in nature. These patterns, however, are repeated throughout the generations, and their intergenerational properties mirror the patterns in our replicating genes.

Practitioners of psychological movements based on somesthetics (meanings encoded in the body and networked with perceptual memory)[27] perform using their breathing, feeling their heartbeats, and using body movements in specific positions and dance algorithms. This allows the sensory consciousness to have a direct perception and authentic experience, not just an intellectual understanding of life. The healing aspect of being encircled in a communal collective deepens rather than expands the morphic field.

The word morphic is of Greek origin and refers to taking a specified shape or form. Rupert Sheldrake, biologist and author of A New Science of Life, understands that memory is inherent in our genes and nature. Sheldrake began the research series for epigenetics, the study of how our genes record and pass on memory, showing that changes in gene expression can be caused by other factors than our DNA. The term epigenesist has been around since C.H. Waddington in 1942 referred to it as the combining of genetics and epigenesis. Embryonic cell differentiation in early stages interacts with the surroundings to produce a phenotype.[28] This means that our environment shapes us and that we are not chained to the DNA code, which explains references to miracles or sudden healing occurrences from diseases such as cancer.

The kolo translates into reality the notion that we are shaped by outside influences, not necessarily our genes. There is plasticity in life that provides room for so-called miracles to occur. Good examples of this are identical twins expressing their genetic material differently from each other, which points to the role of the environment in shaping our genes, not genes determining our outcomes. This is described in Sheldrake's identification with most developmental biologists, explaining that "all biological organisms require organization or fields such as biological, developmental, positional fields and morphogenetic fields".[29] Morphic fields are magnificent conductors of the collective consciousness, the synchronic feeling states communicated through our bodies. We have only to remember how it felt to be a part of a movement or at a concert hall with the audience commanding a standing ovation without a single word to understand this principle.

Ernest L. Rossi's research in his book *The Psychobiology of Gene Expression, Neuroscience and Neurogenesis in Hypnosis and the Healing Arts* aptly describes the epigenetic (having external influences on genes) features of the kolo and morphic field by remarking that "genes are turned on in everyday life during significant life events to make messenger RNA (mRNA) that serves as the blueprint for synthesizing new proteins and neurogenesis to encode memory and learning."[30] What is remarkable is that the South Slavic female social collectives practicing the Mesolithic-aged circular kolos knew that the kolo created space and place for intensified learning, encoding memory, and interacting with genes to record important life experiences.

The South Slavic female social collective, in performing the Mesolithic-aged kolos, was engaging in creative play with genetic expression and a synchronic social collective. John Wheeler, a Princeton physicist and friend of Einstein, describes this activity as being in a participatory universe.[31] The four concentric circles of the kolo mirror circular birds' nests and tree rings as well as our own biological organization. This is the main factor in laying the cards down in four concentric circles, or kolos, as you do a reading. The same morphic field occurs in a circle, dancing the kolo or in a collective.

This same scientific process occurs in cup readings, as we use our genetically- inherited memories to perform ancient tasks. For cup readings, we peer down into the cups. Now, place an image of the four concentric circles onto the cups. Add the overlay of mapping the cup with four pie slices. The cup map reflects the distinctive categories found in South Slavic female social collective practices. Cup readings are a global, holistic methodology that understands that everything in the cosmos, the Earth, and humanity is intimately connected.

Blood and Honey Icons are the kolos experiencing geosynchronous orbits in the circular structure of the round dance pattern. I describe the term geosynchronous orbit as the satellite orbits at approximately 35,800 kilometers above the equator. Objects travel at the same speed as the Earth and thus remain in a stationary position with reference to the Earth; their period of rotation is synchronous with that of the Earth. The categories found in the pie chart map of the cups replicate a geosynchronous circular learning process from simple to complex and serve as a blueprint for learning.

The same occurs when using the Blood and Honey Icons either as a daily practice or at regular intervals for interpreting the messages and meaningfulness of the icons in your life experiences. In cup readings, the geosynchronous orbits, or seasons, are four pie wedges, known as Gromoviti znaci, or Proto-Slavic thunder mark ideograms from the icons placed on houses for protection from lightning bolts. Below is a chart to help you visualize this map to be placed on top of the four concentric Kolo avenues.

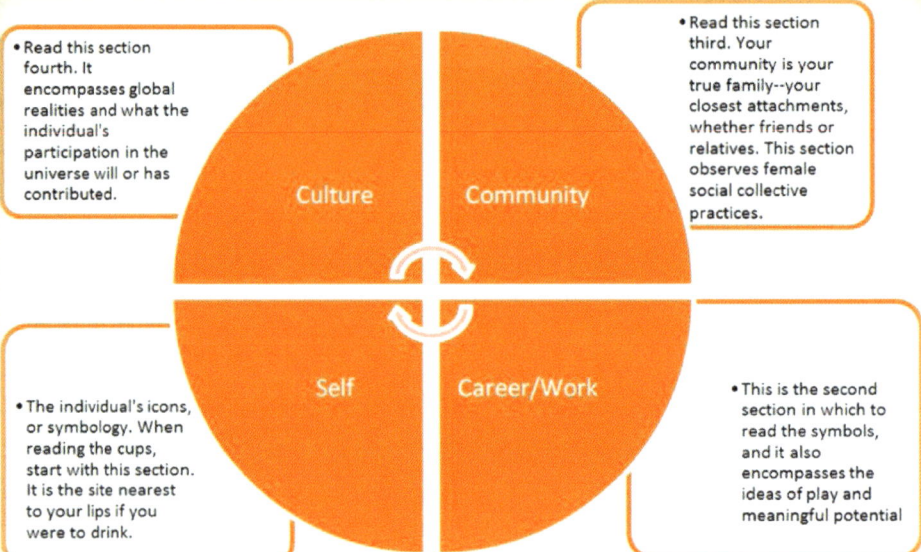

The Cup Map

The Nest/Kolo and Dendrology/Circles: How to Cluster the Meanings

The Nest = kolo = Dendrology/Circles

The nest is but the kolo and is metaphorically represented in dendrology, where the living tree records the environment in its tree rings. Slavic archeomythologies point to epigenetics, where our environment and our life experiences are recorded in our bodies through our DNA and passed down through the generations.

- Dendrology: four concentric circles representing the energy of spatial emptiness and the vacuum at quantum levels
- The kolo, the home—*domovi* means the home of the ancestors in Serbo-Croatian—for the four avenues.
- The nest provides a space and place within seasonal Mother Nature cycles.

The nest/kolo is a dendrology of female culture. To cluster meanings involves the female's ability to evolve the species by repeating truths and life experiences encountered in her migrations. Literally, like tree rings, the nest is constantly layered with new materials and memories. Clustering the meanings takes in the signs, dreams, life experiences, or any material to be placed in the nest/kolo's concentric circles. What occurs when we cluster the meanings is a symbolic map, or orientation to the present moment.

Slavs worship trees and their dendrology. The Slavic observation that trees are fixed in one spot for their entire lifetime, wholly nested into the Earth with their roots and branches that intertwine with the sky, houses their tree of life mythologies.[32]

The sister kinship that Slavs have with the forests underscores this destiny as the ultimate potential of bearing witness, the ultimate meaningfulness of clustering life experiences. The tree rings, kolos, and cups are a mega-library exactly like DNA mitochondria, leaving an authentic, truth-baring record of each migration and life experience.

Migration can occur as we learn in leaps and bounds about a subject of interest or in actual migratory behaviors such as life experiences found in moving away from home, living in other countries, or a simple daily walk at a park or skipping at the ocean shore.

To cluster the meaning of the nest and have an immediate knowledge of the Proto-South-Slavic Moist Mother Earth indicates a dendrology in which we can read the concentric circles of life just as we can with the study of tree rings. We automatically cluster meaning as we interpret signs, messages, and dreams. What is meaningful to us in how life events inspire synchronicity is articulated through our own interpretations.

The greater the diversity in interpretations, the greater the truth posited. The closer we get to witnessing first person stories, not just in this present generation but from the foundational generations of the prehistoric past, the closer we get to revealing that it does not matter where you have been but where you choose to grow, to be, and to witness. Just as no two snowflakes or fingerprints are alike, interpretations leave a visible memory from which to transform ourselves as our ancients have, both biologically and genetically.

The four avenues of the kolo are uroboric, reflecting a circular sense of time. In practicing the kolo, we circle the circle, repeating in each of the four kolo avenues each new life experience. The endless repetition occurs not just in our life experiences but in our genes, our female biology which is passed down through our mitochondria. Mitochondria is passed down through unbroken genetic strings from mother to daughter and is how geneticists trace our origins to our first mother in middle Africa. Placing your randomly chosen cards on the circles, or kolo avenues, provides direction within the circular pursuit of time. References to recipes can also ignite an understanding that archetypal movements are "edible" in the sense that they are ingested and metabolized into practices, or deepened ways of geosynchronous knowing. We can see this with the foods eaten in Mexico or tropical climates of the world having hot spices or peppers in their diet, as hot spices ward off infections and encourage sweating, which cools the body.

If you have observed birds who return to fashion their nests, you understand that the text of a bird's life lies in the exquisitely arranged nest. The small bird repeatedly carries bits and pieces of what most would call scraps or garbage to her home until the nest forms a masterpiece. The masterpiece of the newly created nest cradles new life and symbolizes the narrative of life experiences, including supposedly mundane or ordinary repetitive acts such as those needed to build the nest.

Much of Slavic wisdom, especially that of the South Slavs of the former Yugoslavia, refers clearly to the Neolithic "Old Europe" that appears in the research of Marija Gimbutas. Archeological artifacts have shown that the worship of the Bird Goddess and Goddesses of Regeneration were widespread, and even now, in the modern day, the migration of birds is revered by the Slavs and seen as the essential uroboric kolo, the reflection of native South Slavic harmony with and within nature.

An old legend speaks of three separate Baltic or Slavic tribes originating with the brothers Cech, Lech, and Rus. The eponymous *troikas* (Slavic for three) were responsible for the migration to new lands; Poland is known as Lechia, Bohemia or Cechy refers to the Czech Republic, and Ruthenia or Belorussia became Russia. The legend originated in the story of the three brothers coming upon a white eagle, the Bird Goddess, and her nest.

Coinciding with the legend and fables about the Kolo's thirteen schools of intensified learning, the masculine in the old legend bespeaks a day-to-day existence that honors the feminine, reveres and respects the Moist Mother Earth and seeks to protect her, and more importantly, seeks new learning constantly. Cech, Lech, and Rus met the White Bird Goddess, the same deity to whom Robert Graves refers in his book The White Goddess. Graves states that all men need to learn from and respect the feminine within themselves and all females. *The White Goddess* is the ultimate Kolo, representing the thirteen schools of intensified learning as an instructress for males to fold into harmony with Mother Nature. Females already have this capacity, as shown through their menstruation, pregnancy, and other physical cycles.

Essentially, the Blood and Honey book is the nest. The nest, or the kolo, is a material receptacle layered by your life experiences and how you are connected to all others' life experiences, past and present. This layered nest takes on aspects of quantum psychology clearly and easily, just as it has done for over four thousand years.

The kolo avenues have designated Paleolithic and Neolithic motifs, a mnemonic that is helpful to signal the processes found in each of the avenues. The motifs are shown below with the corresponding kolo avenues.

Circle, Oval 	Arrows, strokes 	Branches, feathers 	Chevrons, zigzag 
Kolo avenue one: element = earth, trust. Direction: South Left	Kolo avenue two: element = fire, remembering. Direction-Meaning: East Eastward-rising life light-right	Kolo avenue three: element = air, gestation. Direction-Meaning: West sunset, womb	Kolo avenue four: element = water, integration. Direction-Meaning: North fixed orientation to truth

Blood and Honey Meta-Definitions: Overview

It is within the book's archetypal movements found in the Blood and Honey Icons that we can orient ourselves into an influential study about ourselves, our social relations, and our environment. The meta-definitions provided in the Blood and Honey Icons pedagogy incorporate past and present memory within a somesthetic foundation.

Placement of the icons or archetypal movement in the nest/kolo begins to cluster the archetypal meanings into sentences. We can capture the essence of our current movements or migrations in our life movements and life experiences that ultimately change us. Migration here refers to movement through our lives and into the life experiences of our ancestors as we learn more about the Blood and Honey Icons and perform card and cup readings. For instance, if you randomly selected the Fish Goddess (Whirlpools and Spirals) Icon from the Blood and Honey Icon cards or from the ebook and printed book, you will see in its summary evoked collective consciousness focused on oceans and rivers, which are spirals that represent life and death, and caves, suggesting the incubation of life. Since the Blood and Honey Icon of the Fish Goddess (Whirlpools and Spirals) belongs in kolo avenue four, as noted on the card, we include its directions and meanings when we make interpretations such as:

- The meanings found in the summary, icon cards, and archetypal movement are in tandem with your first person story—your life experiences—and linked to your perceptual memory.

- The expression of the iconic materials and symbols refers to the process that returns us to the moment and speaks volumes about how you have evolved, migrated, or grown.

Looking at Avenue Four's representational features, with the motif of 〰〰, we situate the meaning of the card within the symbols of winter, maturity, the sunset, and the womb, suggesting the commingling of all life experiences as an integration process. Reflect on which symbolic representations of the Blood and Honey Icon card of the Fish Goddess (Whirlpools and Spirals) you respond to. Now combine your responses with your first person story. Determine what your card means for you specifically according to your life experiences through the lens of the symbolic representations within the Blood and Honey Icon card of the Fish Goddess (Whirlpools and Spirals) and your first person story.

The Fish Goddess card can bring to light life experiences ranging from the death of a relationship to ways in which your childhood brought new life to the people around you. Remember that you are always the final interpreter of your life, dreams, symbolic events, and messages. If your card reading is a simple equation of meaning, then you are the one who writes down what goes after the equal sign; you determine the meaning of the symbolic materials you find based on what they prompt in you according to your life experiences.

Pulling additional cards or archetypal movements from the book will only add more depth and space for you to evolve. Adding your first person stories to the meanings listed on the card opens up your own unique life experiences and merges them with South Slavic archetypal energies and directions.

Use of the lexicon of South Slavic female culture symbols listed for the Blood and Honey Icons material deepens the meanings associated with your first person stories. Use them along with the cards to cluster more meaning into your own life events and experiences.

Meta Definitions

We start with Archetypal Movements, referring to the Blood and Honey Icons. Archetypal movements include each of these fields: evolutionary biology, psycho-biological psychology, quantum psychology, somatic psychology, somesthetics, and scientific practice. Combining all of these fields as avenues for studying the Blood and Honey Icons leads directly to nonlinguistic emotional meanings stored in our bodies and networked with our neurological perceptual memories.

The Blood and Honey Icons book contains specific icons such as Storied Aprons and a host of other icons that prompt experiential archetypal movement, a discipline in which everything is connected and interrelated. Archetypes are inherited thought, original models of using human senses as the pathways for intensified learning. The patterns resulting from archetypes are the origins of all types of representation. The archetypal movements circle experiential senses, just as dancers circle through the kolo, to identify meanings and to open perspectives often resisted or buried out of fear. Fear keeps the individual fixated in the same spot, repeating the same actions and halting any depth work.

A good example of depth work is daily life, which is a series of repeated acts, including eating, sleeping, performing domestic tasks, and going to work, where many of us spend almost two-thirds of our time. If we repeat our life experiences in fear of losing our jobs or marginalization, such as the resentment that comes when one person performs all domestic tasks for the family, anger or rage will surely follow. We are stuck in repeating the same old pattern of fear. However, if we repeat the daily life practices with awe, curiosity, and as intensified learning situations, the repetition layers a new memory over the old, fostering adaptive skills and resiliency skills. We are not going through motions numbly or with fear but rather allowing for plasticity in our domestic life and work, which ushers in positive change.

The reorientation needed for inspiring wisdom with healing harmony takes place within the archetypal movement references in the kolo avenues.

What seems unrelated at first gains meaning and thus progresses to awareness. The kolo avenues in the archetypal movement function like recipes, directing the archetypes— inherited thought— toward awareness or insight.

Scientists still have not been able to figure out how we learn through our senses. For the past two thousand years, thinkers from Plato to Noam Chomsky have argued that memory and even abstract and seemingly impossible complex mathematical concepts such as space and time are present in the human mind from birth. It stands to reason that the universal component is our bodies and neurological systems— our brains. All of us have this archetypal imprint of the basic understanding of the world and our minds. Anything we have learned is because of our life experiences, the life experiences of our ancestors, and how we participate in these events.

Yet, teaching in most academic areas is limited to linear materials and logical appropriations that remove the senses and the body from the coursework. Somesthetics, with its nonlinguistic and proto-linguistic communications, essentially communicates via proto-symbolic forms. Archetypal material is processed according to our bodily senses, and its intricate neurological network links to perceptual memory. Iconic representations and symbols are taken in and understood through the hard-wiring already present in our bodies and brains.

Neuroscientist Efrat Ginot calls the autonomic neurological responses such as breathing, dreaming, and even blood pressure the non-conscious rather than the unconscious.[33] In other words, our bodies do these important functions without our thinking about it, yet our bodies will react and respond to the environment and intense affective states. These feelings can prompt an increase in blood pressure or the release of the stress hormones adrenaline and cortisol better than any medical or pharmaceutical intervention.

We tend to ignore these non-linguistic and non-conscious communications. Ginot's research probes the conscious language of the left brain with the proto-symbolic representation of the right brain, a non-conscious, autonomic communication. Ginot states that the proto-symbolic right brain is dissociated as a result of childhood or traumatic events but becomes a space to enable intersubjectivity, where diverse subjects and opinions coincide, and for neural networks to move toward integration. First person stories and narratives allow for integration and meaningfulness to transcribe a new memory over a traumatic event.

The fundamental way in which nonlinguistic communications operate is through mirror neurons, which are both critical for learning and the neural networks of the earliest attachment approaches. In the earliest attachment phases, feeling states are honed by both the infant and the mother. Mirror neurons are known to prompt neural connections or neural plasticity for the developing brain. The infant is much more observant than most realize. The same is true of our bodies, which can act like plasma computers, soaking in more information than we are conscious of. The non- linguistic and non-conscious involvement describes archetypal movements and the impact of the Blood and Honey Icons pedagogy.

We are erroneously trained to think that answers are the solution to seek, when life is more about evolving and intensified learning than resolving questions. When we think about it, solving is mostly the left brain's conscious language. However, we do not need to devalue or throw away our invaluable linear and logical conscious language. Developing a sense of rhythm as to when, where, and how to include the linear and logical conscious language is useful once we have processed and are learning intensely about our non-linguistic and non-conscious symbolic and iconic communications.

Coupling conscious language with non-conscious proto-symbolic language evolves our archetypal movements, producing the material found in our own Blood and Honey Icons. Ever-evolving and universal properties found in the specific archetypes become personalized according to each person's unique life experiences.

Remember how difficult it was to learn how to ride a bike, roller blade, or ice skate without falling? Years later, we can get on that bike without difficulty. Since the body understands the proto-symbolic language, a dance algorithm or movement pattern emerges. When we look to define or at least approach archetypal movement, we would note that the inherited thought-idea-prototype of the archetype partners with movement, which opens the senses to intensified learning. Movement suggests both things and actions--nouns and verbs. It indicates both the flowing river and the flow itself, operating as an archetype for water. The kolo avenues or directions are metaphors to experience the kolo dance pattern within the concept of archetypal movement.

Write down the archetypal movements (Blood and Honey Icons) that you are drawn to and reflect on where the Blood and Honey Icons are placed on the nest-dendrology of concentric kolo avenue circles. The Blood and Honey practices prompt first person stories (storied instructions) to litter and thereby build the nest, increasing the abundance found in evolving from resting in what is or what you have known to embracing the unknown. Rarely do we find ourselves embracing the unknown; we prefer the familiar, but we remain fixated and stuck if we do not embrace intensified learning, not through catastrophic trauma and manmade violence but by our need to grow, expand, and evolve. Becoming comfortable with being uncomfortable in not seeking answers or problem solving is at heart here.

The Bioculinary as Applied Kinesiology

Blood and Honey's bioculinary aspect is inscribed in the memory of Slavic agrarian festivals that reflected the transmutation of life and death into the service of the Moist Mother Earth.[34] The observance of feminine growth and maturation, based on the cyclical seasons of the earth, is rarely studied. In Blood and Honey, we observe the metaphoric and symbolic Great Mother, or Slavic Moist Earth, as "interwoven into the very fabric of agricultural rites, celebrating birth, marriage, and death in nature and by analogy in the community." Bioculinary practice is self-sustainability without impacting future generations except to enhance natural productivity and fertility practices. The reality is that our bodies' biological, genetic processes are Paleolithic, if not older.

In Blood and Honey Icons pedagogy, we learn about ancient South Slavic practices regarding flora, fauna, foods, and herbs through the recipes found in most of the Blood and Honey Icons. Recipes, both ancient and modern, represent the life cycle, suggesting how we inherit materiality from the seed, so tiny that it barely dots the swirl on a fingerprint but can turn into blooming tomato plants.

The senses involved in the bioculinary, from the aroma of cooking food and the smell of earth after a soft rain to tasting the harvest we planted, symbolize a progression of events that we caused to occur with our bioculinary practices. The simplest of gardens, even container gardens of herbs, are also included in this process. The cook appreciates and pays homage to the herbs or fruits requiring thousands of hours of sunlight, literally tons of water, and the minerals in the soil.

We have not been successful in converting Paleolithic biological and genetic functions to modern-day sedentary lifestyles and processed food consumption. Our ancient agrarian practices, now submerged under a tidal wave of gleaming metal combines, corporate farms, and seedless produce owned and patented by business concerns, seem to have disappeared. In the aftermath of yet another war on former Yugoslav soil, the people returned to agrarian Neolithic practices in order to survive and to be self-sustained. It was as if the collective memories rose up in the farmer's hands once she immersed them in the moist dirt.

Agrarian practices operating only over a few generations since WWII for the South Slavs changed dramatically due to the brutal war in the 1990s. A common sight in Bosnia includes women tilling the soil, tossing seeds, and raking. Bioculinary arts like churning butter as their great grandmothers did and roasting lamb in round- bellied fireplaces fed by dead wood found in their thick forests create a picturesque if not commemorative Neolithic landscape. Bioculinary practices embody collective memory, manifesting a dynamic challenge between the home and the cosmos so that an intimate and serious study of South Slavic dwelling spaces and places imparts long-term remembering.

Bioculinary practices in specific archetypal chapter movements (Blood and Honey Icons) contain South Slavic recipes, most of which the women held onto during the war's sieges and sniper firing in the past three wars. Bioculinary practices for the South Slavs and the Balkans are important because of logographical and iconic outcomes—in other words, the recipes go beyond words in that they map a return to Neolithic practices that are in proper relation to the earth, sky, air, and water.

Bioculinary practices give us biographical information about Paleolithic and Neolithic ancients' experiential approaches to domestic dwelling, agriculture, and husbandry, offering an analysis of their intimate lives. Slavs' discovery that memories are motionless and therefore reachable in the present day allows them to focus on social rituals and practices as the method to ensure the presence of ancestral collective memories in times of great need, as well as for regular evolution within our daily lives. Motionless memories can be understood through the metaphor of photographs in an album. Yellowing might occur, but the picture is frozen in time and place for us to remember.

The sheer volume of bioculinary practices, including the recipes found in the Blood and Honey archetypal movements, actually threads the concentrated collective memory from the Paleolithic and Neolithic "Old Europe" agrarian way of life. South Slavic women from days long ago have inscribed within their cellular memories a pharmacy and storehouse of relations between the land, botany, agriculture, and healthy bodies.

The recipes are not typical of cookbooks. The recipes invite you to have organic food within a 150-mile radius of your home or to grow your own food. After each war in the former Yugoslav region, women often had to feed their families from what they could grow in rusty tin cans or discarded plastic tubs. The tiniest of balconies fed whole families while providing medicinal or herbal remedies.

What remains of their bioculinary practices is perhaps a distant cousin of the diet and lifestyle of my ancient South Slavic grandmothers, but it is all that I have at this point. Three wars in one century managed to destroy much of the South Slavic female social collective's concentrated memory, or ties with their Moist Mother Earth. The intangible heritage of the South Slavic female social collective is invisible, just as female labor, concentrated within the home, often goes unseen.[36] Sociologist Marjorie DeVault, in her construction of gender and family through food practices, determined that "women quite literally produce family life from day to day."[37]

Our culinary dishes are the result of thousands of years of foraging, agricultural pursuits, and nutritional needs. To separate the culinary arts as being domestic in value and apart from the natural sciences has caused a severed relationship between our bodies and our earthly environment. This separation impacts the fields of paleoecology (inter-relations of the prehistoric life and environments), paleoclimatology (prehistoric climates on a global or regional scale from evidence preserved in glacial deposits, sedimentary structures, and fossils), palynology (the study of spores and pollen), and ethnobotany (plant remains from archaeological contexts and the uses of plants in female culture and context).

Specific references to Paleolithic and Neolithic uses of various plants in recipes that were handed down through the generations and are still in use today are found throughout the Blood and Honey Icons. Pursuing an understanding of past bioculinary practices opens us up to somatic consciousness of healing and revitalizing our health despite adverse conditions

Paleolithic and Neolithic Motifs and Core Signs as Iconic, Non-linguistic Representation

Motifs are reoccurring patterns. Thematic elements in literary forms and the artistic or esthetic forms, motifs coalesce into a central, core idea. Iconic and purely mnemonic principles identifying nature's motifs and core signs have a profound ability to invoke immediate understanding without our uttering a single word.

For example, four South Slavic motifs in shapes and forms traced to the Upper Paleolithic Period are often found on South Slavic aprons, blouses, ceramics, and artwork such as:

Four South Slavic Paleolithic and Neolithic Motifs

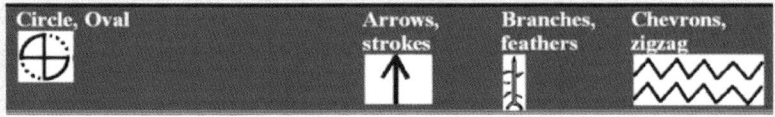

The Paleolithic and Neolithic motifs are paired with the kolo avenues and their iconic representations. A closer look at the Paleolithic and Neolithic Motifs reveals the implications of a symbol's potency in multiple memories that reside in its form, just as a picture is said to speak a thousand words.

Note how the fixed memory in Paleolithic and Neolithic motifs does not carry the same fixed meaning as modern South Slavic embroidered linens or textiles. Yet, it remains in the same motif form, thereby containing multiple meanings, adding on to the ancestoral memory. The reason for this is the fact that every single one of the present day female's life experiences is layered onto the Paleolithic and Neolithic Motifs. Unfortunately, this same process can occur in the negative, such as Hilter's reappropriation of the swastika, which originally meant life and the sun, as a tool of war and hatred.

What is Evoked through Collective Memory:

Researchers using paleolingustic, paleoethnological, and paleomythological materials study the Paleolithic and Neolithic symbols and motifs not as a writing alphabet but as an alphabet performing as a script of incised signs or symbols with much broader meanings. A script for a play or movie has within its narrative an array of feeling states, postures, and body movements, symbolized variously to convey immediate meaning through such indicators as a raised eyebrow or hands cupped over the face. The indigenous early Eneolithic and Neolithic scripts found in the former Yugoslav region are thousands of years old and definitely not represented in contemporary alphabetic writing.[38] This indicates an exclusion of the soma and our neurological communication that is performed mostly in iconic movements and symbolic forms. Evoked collective memory speaks of the communal memories built through the generations.

It is interesting to note that almost all of the archeological evidence for this was found in a house setting (*domovi* in Serb-Croatian is the home of the ancestors) and household areas, including storage and garbage pits. Through Paleolithic and Neolithic motifs, we examine the life experiences and daily practices of a people who did not separate the body from the mind or spirit. Domestic life and communal living developed a meaningful system for the intergenerational flow of information, which evokes collective memory.

Paleolithic and Neolithic Motif: Kolo Avenue one (Trust and Earth)

The circle, oval, teardrop, uterus-vulva-seed shape, and triangles are associated with the sacred journeys of all females through the chakras, known as the seven nerve centers of the body. Circling down through the chakras is related to the female life stages of menstruation, childbirth, and menopause. Men circle up through the chakras to gain discipline and higher cognitive functioning. Circling either up or down through chakras or nerve centers portrays the intensified learning of our biological processes.

The circle motifs and downward-pointing triangles indicate the uterus, the only organ absent from the male body. The location of the uterus in the symbolism of the circle is significant because of the extraordinary feat of gestation and childbirth, the same feat performed by Moist Mother Earth as seeds are planted and take root. These are downward motions, from bringing a child into the world to planting a seed that puts roots into the soil, and each requires fertilization, care, and nurturing into growth.

The triangles pointing down represent female pubic growth, while triangles pointing up suggest male pubic growth. The location of the male triangle indicates upward movement through the chakras. The triangle shapes designated in the circle motif express growth and repeated migration toward abundance within the entire context of the Neolithic motifs, signaling a return to South Slavic Moist Mother Earth and the healing arts.

The circle motif is womb-centered with a seed matrix that generates potency and accesses self-sustaining energy found within. Traced from the ideograms of the Upper Paleolithic, womb-seed symbols can be observed today as the Magdalenian disks and concentric circles of halos around Christian saints and angels. The body is iconic of communal living, having intimate close relations of space and place through spatial position, body postures, and sensory contact that provide social identity to living collectives.[39]

These South Slavic shapes and forms are associated with kolo avenue one (elements: Earth, trust; direction: south). Movement toward the south is called the left in a circular path. The south is a place of depth and breadth, becoming specialized and expert at your passion. Somesthetic sensations and being grounded in the body facilitate understanding within the physical domain.

Iconic representation of kolo avenue one are found in the bottom of the cup or the interior of the kolo circle. Earth and trust are reference frames to strengthen and embrace those around us and receive the same in return. Trust cannot belong exclusively outside ourselves or our bodies. Having trust in ourselves includes trusting that the seasons and the earth will always remain.

Trust is housed neurologically with safety in the temporal lobes via the hippocampus and the amygdala.[40] The temporal lobes form new memories, translating significant emotional and feeling states to enable us to determine what actions we should take based on events that have occurred in our lives. Trust is an intensive learning process for acquiring new and relevant information.

Kolo avenue one contains the somatic consciousness for the affective/feeling states of trust in body intimacy. What is earth to you? How have you come to be intimate with trust? Sensorimotor activities like dancing the kolo in bare feet in the grass or massaging your hands and feet are coherent examples of the power of being in kolo avenue one.

If you pull the Storied Aprons Blood and Honey Icon card for kolo avenue one, you must think about the power of doubling, such as in pregnancy, and of your connection to others, a social collective originating in the womb, home, and community. Review the South Slavic female symbols and cultural humanities, observing whether any of the four patterns of shapes and forms listed on the Storied Aprons card appear in your life experiences. Which one speaks most to you?

After you have had a significant dream, a Jungian dream analyst would ask you to perform a task pertaining to the material of the dream, such as burying a letter or tossing a flower into the ocean if a similar event took place in the dream-state. Qabbalists regard the earth as "one great magnet" that can induce an inflowing power.[41] You may feel the need to use the Blood and

Honey Icon pedagogy cards or cup readings in the same fashion. For the cup readings, search in the grounds or tea leaves for any of the forms listed.

For kolo avenue one, we are centered in the home. As we have discussed, the home, or *domovi* in Serbo-Croatian, means the residence of the ancestors, but we can also consider this our DNA, the literal residence of the remnants of our genetic ancestors. In cup readings, the bottom of the cup is always the home/*domovi*. Please include the Paleolithic and Neolithic Motif and Core Signs to prompt a storied instruction or direction in your life.

The Storied Aprons Icon within kolo avenue one represents our skill in clustering symbolic messages into meaningfulness, sensorimotor (movements), affective or neurological regulation, and formal linguistic expression.

For cup readings, visualize the symbolic references found in tea leaves or grounds within kolo avenue one at the bottom of the cup. Apply the pie chart map of cup readings. As in a card reading, this reveals our skill in clustering symbolic messages into meaningfulness, sensorimotor (movements), affective or neurological regulation, and formal linguistic expression.

Paleolithic and Neolithic Motif: Kolo Avenue Two (Remembering and Fire)

Arrows, single strokes, double strokes, claviforms, and the letters X and Y symbolize surrendering to the energies that reveal our interconnectedness to all living things. Double strokes and the letter X refer to gestating, redoubling, and the ability to hold the tension between polar opposites, which is life energy. The arrow is associated with ritual, ceremony, and wounding. The Y references the clan mother in genetics and indicates a mother with two daughters. The symbolic arrows, single strokes, claviforms, and the letters X and Y point to abundance and the power of two.

In the earliest forms of writing, pictograms combined the representations of objects to express an idea. Clay tablets were used to record the script, with women, the first potters, giving way to a material repository for symbolic language.[42] At Susa, during the Neolithic period, stones with geometric designs were used for counting using single strokes.[43] Thirteen single strokes appear on a bison horn held by a full-bodied prehistoric female figure called the Laussel Goddess, representing the thirteen lunar months that mirror the menstrual cycle. The artifact is carbon dated at 22,000 years old and indicates that the origin of mathematics is in female menstrual cycles.[44]

Kolo avenue two uses the elements of fire and remembering as its geocentric reference frame. Fire is associated with the somatic affect of pain, not only burning away what no longer is needed but providing inspiration and profound energy. Memory is experienced not as ego but as embodied archaeologies of memory that have evolved human society and our communal way of life. By the same token, fire illuminates and provides insight.

Jungian analyst Ester Harding writes about the perpetual fire at Tara, where Irish kings were crowned, or the festivals of Midsummer Eve and Beltane, but she specifically points to the thread of Paleolithic and Neolithic female social collectives found in the Moon Goddess temples with a perpetual sacred fire present in Eastern and Orthodox Serb, Russian, and Greek churches where the most important ceremonies of the year center around new light on Easter Sunday.[45] The observance of a repeating pattern of new light at the spring equinox points to the geocentric charting of the sun and the seasons of the Earth.

Fire and remembering are concerned with female social collectives and their domestic art, which leads to an exploration of a South African find of Acheulian tools dating from about 1.5 million years ago and made of burned cobbles and bones.[46] It took another million years of constant intergenerational practice with fires, as culinary practices and for warmth, before hearths and fireplaces were found in archeological remains.[47] When the Storied Aprons card is placed in kolo avenue two, it points to the need for insight, awareness, and reflection on memories, not as a burden but as a learning process.

For the card interpretations and cup readings, the concentric circle second from the bottom is kolo avenue two. Kolo avenue two is iconic of the hearth, or *pech* in Serbo-Croatian. The use of fire within the *pech* in essence provided a sacred *domovi* for new light among South Slavic peoples. According to Marija Gimbutas, symbols of the sun from Old Europe (Neolithic) and Indo-European mythologies are manifestations of the feminine and are noted in the Slavic languages inherited from Old Europe.[48]

The Anza site in the Ovce Polje area, in the Neolithic-era former Yugoslavia, reflects Starcevo culture and is an ecological haven established around 6300-6200 BCE.[49] North of Greece, the timber *domovi* have long since returned to the earth. Gimbutas noted that ritual burning of the homes was performed at this site. We can only infer symbolically the real reason for home-torching rituals. Fire brings purification, a burning away of diseases, violence, and memories that do not serve the purpose of living in harmony.

Could fire alternatively represent a burning of new memories, skills, and intensified learning environments that are passed down through the generations? Memes, the cultural intergenerational transmission of life experiences that shape our DNA and survival skills, are examples of burning new memories as if the brain were a CD. Flashes of brilliance or insight, memes have helped us evolve as a species, for better or for worse.

Our sun is responsible for a wide range of effects on our bodies and minds. Measuring brain activity is basically recording electrical activity. Geocentric organizations of the kolo in kolo avenue two focus on geomagnetic properties such a magnetic storm or solar flares disrupting or burning out our communications on a global basis. These can also cause havoc in our neurological systems, leading to an increase in mental disorders. Joan Didion recorded this phenomenon in her celebrated essay "Los Angeles Notebook" in the collection *Slouching Toward Bethlehem*. According to Didion, significant, empirically verified instances of mental disorders and violent behavior coincide with the advent of the Santa Ana winds. Though people receive no tangible warning, their behavior nonetheless changes dramatically under this invisible influence.

When you are doing a cup reading based on kolo avenue two, search in the cup for any solar symbols, such as life-giving icons suggesting the ancient archeomythologies of the god of the Shining Sky, a god who changes based on the time of year, from the birthing of the sun to the young sun in spring, the triumphant sun in summer, and the old sun in autumn.

The Storied Aprons Icon within kolo avenue two represents our skill in clustering symbolic messages into meaningfulness, sensorimotor (movements), affective or neurological regulation, and formal linguistic expression.

For cup readings, visualize the symbolic references found in tea leaves or grounds within kolo avenue two, at the bottom of the cup. Apply the pie chart map of cup readings. As in a card reading, this reveals our skill in clustering symbolic messages into meaningfulness, sensorimotor (movements), affective or neurological regulation, and formal linguistic expression. Kolo avenue two, with these universal Paleolithic shapes and forms, is connected to the elements of fire and remembering, and the relevant direction is east, or a right-side orientation of the body. Kolo avenue two is a circular path that leads us to begin anew, to wake at dawn to experience the purest moments of the day. Moving towards the right is often indicated.

Paleolithic and Neolithic Motif: Kolo Avenue Three (Air and Gestation)

Branches, feathers, trees, rectangles with lines in them, open ellipses, and birthing images speak of the message to give birth, to grow, to sprout and unfold. Schematized Neolithic graffiti shows the designs of an ancient system to express what cannot be seen, only known. At Windmill Hill in central Germany (TRB culture 4th millennium BCE) "near perfect circles, ellipses, or egg shapes [were found that] are related to the Pythagorean triangle two thousand years before Pythagoras," attesting to women's menstruation cycles as the true origin of mathematics.[51] Eggs are prominent shapes and forms for kolo avenue three's elements of air and gestation; the direction is west, which describes a circular path moving towards the sunset, the completion and celebration of your journeys at the end of the day.

The concentric circle to focus on in a reading using kolo avenue three is the third from the bottom of the cup. The kolo's concentric circles are geocentric reference points leading to the manifestation of creativity as it becomes creation. Another significant feature is that geocentric approaches allow us to understand how we are all related and interconnected. The main feature of our earthly environment is elegantly simple. Let's take a look at oxygen in our atmosphere and how it is tied to trees. We do know that trees feed on carbon dioxide, thereby creating oxygen for us to breathe. Despite knowing this critical factor, we continue our worldwide destruction of forests unabated.

Fire cannot be fed without oxygen, no matter how combustible the materials involved. Perhaps air, with its invisibility and transparency, is difficult to express or honor for its sacred properties to which life clings.

To date, no drug is available to treat Post Traumatic Stress Disorder. No known talking therapies for trauma can outperform taking a breath, or a breather. Taking a breath, a pause, calms the nervous system, specifically the para-sympathetic nervous system (PNS) if it is triggered by threat, violence, fear, or anxiety.[52] For that matter, movement of the body in the kolo dance or sports activities reduces the adrenaline and cortisol coursing through our bodies when we are stressed by traumatic events.

Air is divinity and life, an uncomplicated, immediate knowing, while gestation is the somatic affect, or feeling state, of living in ambiguity—being neither here or there. Pregnancy is also a period of vulnerability that needs to be supported and nurtured. Air and gestation are about giving birth to embodied forms. Breath practices and well-balanced stances or postures found in the kolo, performed sensitively, thoughtfully, and joyfully, can prompt an attitudinal change that increases transparency and authenticity.

Many individuals mention having great ideas in the shower or when walking their faithful canine companions. It seems that, when we are moving and breathing in the moment, not in a state of fear or stress, creative insight comes easily.

The study of the kolo is about following and referencing your own somatically embodied movements, not those of teachers, authority figures, or experts. Gestation is not just female pregnancy; its process is evident and observable in both genders. Males, in manifesting their creativity such as in architecture, engineering, and even coaching, are in this sense pregnant with potential. Yet, on a physical level, males mimic the female's pregnancy features of sleeplessness and weight gain, called sympathetic symptoms. However, the gestating female has an intimate lived wisdom of pregnancy that is important in kolo avenue three. Eric Neumann's work *The Great Mother* posits a basic symbolic equation: "woman = body = vessel, which is the elementary experience of the feminine."[53] Neumann observes the domestic art forms ennobled in ritual and traditional practices found in the female social collective practices, stating, "Food and drink are put into this unknown vessel, while in all creative functions, from the elimination of waste and emission of seed to the giving forth of breath and the word, something is 'born' out of it."[54]

The vast perinatal intricacies and fetal psychology fields are documenting what the South Slavic female social collectives knew millennia ago.[55] The same can be said of most indigenous tribes, which are matrifocal in their organization across the globe. For the South Slavs, maternal fright is both potent and toxic in its propensity to escalate levels of violence, disease, and mental disorders, and repeated studies have shown that the children of traumatized mothers are predisposed to commit violence. Focusing on maternal well-being and loving and honoring the mother both heals her and provides equilibrium to our ever-changing environment.

In the example of the Blood and Honey Icon Storied Aprons card, the apron brings focus to gestation, functioning as a necklace that decorates the womb. Pockets found in most aprons signify the womb and the mitochondrial DNA that is passed unbroken from mother to daughter. Placed in kolo avenue three and its Paleolithic and Neolithic motif, the card can indicate that you are figuratively pregnant, as with ideas and creativity, and that you may bring form to what is immanent (indwelling or inherent) and invisible.

The Storied Aprons Icon placed in kolo avenue three represents our skill in clustering symbolic messages into meaningfulness, sensorimotor movements, affective or neurological regulation, and formal linguistic expression.

If you feel the need to have more description, place the pie chart map of the cup over your dendrology/nest of four concentric kolo avenues where your cards are placed.

For cup readings, visualize the symbolic references found in tea leaves or grounds within kolo avenue three, at the bottom of the cup. Apply the pie chart map of cup readings. As in a card reading, this reveals our skill in clustering symbolic messages into meaningfulness, sensorimotor (movements), affective or neurological regulation, and formal linguistic expression.

Paleolithic and Neolithic Motif: Kolo Avenue Four (Gestation and Water)

Chevrons, zigzags, running angles, groups of three lines, rays (comets), meandering lines, spirals, and arcs represent migrations, or sacred pilgrimages that function as the exploratory movement of living things in the kolo. Marija Gimbutas referred to the ideograms of Vs, zigzags, chevrons, meandering lines, and spirals as signifying water and rain, properties of the Snake and Bird Goddess artifacts strewn about the former Yugoslavian geographical regions.[56] Tree of Life columns in "Old Europe" were encoded with vertically piled arcs and winding snakes.[57] Aquatic ideograms were zigzags, wavy lines, arcs, and cup marks, along with serpents, spirals, horns, axes, and even combs.

Snakes, rivers, and comets are expressions intertwined with kolo avenue four's element of water-integration, and its indicated direction is north. The northern path is circular and condensed, pointing to the true north. The North Star is fixed in the sky, conveying the message that we move toward omniscience throughout life. Stars signify wisdom.

Kolo avenue four depicts the sky, from which the waters of life rain down. Practitioners in the fields of infoceuticals and bioenergetics refer to body-field alignment, or orientation to the earth's vertical, equatorial, and magnetic polar axes, as the Big Field.[58] Atmospheric physicists starting with W. O. Schumann studied resonant cavities and standing waves. Eric Weisstein's *World of Physics* describes the resonant cavity as the place where standing waves are built up.

It is a cavity for electromagnetic waves.⁵⁹ Cavities, like caves, allow the same process to build.

The ionosphere, thirty-four miles above earth, is iconic of kolo avenue four. We can say that a resonant cavity is also where kolo dances are performed. South Slavic kolos have the postures—the vertical, equatorial and polar axes—of an ethnochoreographic practice. Specific folk round dances are for rain, others for the celebratory equinox rituals, and certain algorithmic kolos for specific seasons. The result is an integration of life experiences performed mnemonically throughout the generations.

Horizontal and vertical space weaves somesthetic movements, perhaps in the same fashion as the embroidery of linen or folk costumes. As with the costumes and embroidery of the South Slavic people, the cardinal points of their relations to cosmological space are organized with the Paleolithic and Neolithic motifs and kolo avenues. Their practical immersion in and specific interactions with their environment reflect a shamanic model of the universe from which vital energy flows through their spines, which are thus iconic of the world tree.⁶⁰ This provides an orientation other than that of a map. As a result, the North Pole is the head and the South Pole the feet. The kolo avenues are an orientation and direction of gender- appropriate activities organized around spatial domains.⁶¹

The example of the Blood and Honey Icon Storied Aprons card placed in kolo avenue four indicates full integration of your life experiences with your present circumstances and age-old social memories, the nexus of salient cultural dimensions.

The kolo mnemonically and biosemiotically carries culturally encoded meanings and values. In kolo avenue four, at the rim of the dendrology/nest, the concentric circles of the kolo or the cup indicate that "you are here." Water merges and integrates into all of life and death, as made visible by the Slavic spiral, allowing an unequivocally meaningful somatic circular flow.

The Storied Aprons Icon placed in kolo avenue four represents our skill in clustering symbolic messages into meaningfulness, sensorimotor movements, affective or neurological regulation, and formal linguistic expression. If you feel the need to have more description, place the pie chart map of the cup over your dendrology/nest of four concentric kolo avenues where your cards are placed.

For cup readings, visualize the symbolic references found in tea leaves or grounds within kolo avenue four at the bottom of the cup. Apply the pie chart map of cup readings. As in a card reading, this reveals our skill in clustering symbolic messages into meaningfulness, sensorimotor (movements), affective or neurological regulation, and formal linguistic expression.

South Slavic Female Symbology and Female Humanities: The Healing Arts

In essence, South Slavic female symbology and female humanities are the lost language of symbolism, our mother tongue. Lost but not forgotten, the concentrated collective memory of communal life, with its spiritual and practical applications, dates from between 5,200 BCE and 3,500 BCE.[62] However, the forbidden herstories and rich matrifocal heritage of female humanities beliefs quietly found articulation and expression through the accumulated symbolism in fairytales, mythologies, narrative art, and oral memory traditions. Brought about through the agrarian way of life that centers on South Slavic female hands and bioculinary practices such as the tea and coffee cup readings, this symbology of the feminine is magnified in non-linguistic, non-conscious proto-communications and language.

South Slavic female humanities incorporates tasseography (feminine divining) into ecology and mnemonics. I am convinced that feminine divining is but our bodies' non-linguistic, non-conscious proto-communications and language. Tasseography interprets the patterns left behind in tea leaves, coffee grounds, and wine sediments. The terms derive from the French word *tasse* (cup), which in turn derives from the Arabic *tassa* (cup), and the Greek suffixes -graph (writing), -logy (a subject or study of a subject), and divination. The terms derive from the French word tasse (cup), which in turn derives from the Arabic tassa (cup), and the Greek suffixes -graph (writing) and -logy (a subject or study of a subject). The word divination derives from the Indo-European word deiwos, which is associated with "sky and "day," implying shining. The Latin word deus means 'god,' and diva means 'goddess.' Divinus was used as a noun meaning 'soothsayer.'

A compelling aspect is how the "Old Europe" archeological artifacts provide specific evidence supporting the study of female South Slavic symbology and female humanities. Like a cookery book or gardening tome, South Slavic female symbology and female humanities are comprehensive guides to cultivating one's own mother tongue through the exploration of dreams, tea and coffee cup readings, and our own individual life experiences.

Almost everything we have to date, from archeology to mathematics, is written as his-stories, phallic and male-centered memorials that represent his world and constitute a total eclipse of female symbology. Icons and female humanities are consistently excluded from society, the sciences, and females themselves. The failure to incorporate female accounts cannot intensify learning modes that are richly present in the mother/child bond and attachment development. I do not recommend obliterating the masculine account; instead, *Blood and Honey* looks to mitigate the imbalance by delving into and making a space for female South Slavic symbology and female humanities.

One of the most concrete sensory experiences resulting from birthing and nurturing a child is the development of an amazingly deep, abstract, and complex understanding of our world; women's learning capacities are the greatest untold story and perhaps the most devalued. Psychological and sociological studies reveal the primacy of the mother, not only in raising a child but in evolving a community; maternal neglect, for example, stunts a child in the learning process, cutting out curiosity, interest, awe, and wonder.

The prolific damage done by excluding female symbology and female humanities on the basis of supposed inferiority to male symbology and humanities can be observed in the catastrophic violence that is commonplace in our headline news. Female South Slavic symbology and female humanities take in a script that ennobles female life experiences and is central to self-sustainability issues, from which we could learn instead to heal from and subvert violence, breaking the seemingly endless, intergenerational cycle of violence that we have witnessed for so long.

In modern life, we can barely remember more than one generation back, let alone a text message we wrote on our BlackBerry phones an hour ago. Denial of past holocausts and gynocides allows masculine perspectives to dominate, relegating the woman's response to the fear of being victimized. Such a one-sided flow of information led Lynn Margulis, a researcher-scientist who traced our origins from mere bacteria and was once married to Carl Sagan, to reveal in her book *Symbiosis* that the privileging of masculine perspectives is a "trained incapacity" into which we are all indoctrinated.

Female South Slavic symbology and female humanities appear in each archetypal chapter of the Blood and Honey Icons and constitute a collection, if not a collectivized, memory handed down through the ages. The pervasive theme is how thousands of generations of female life experiences are remembered in the present generation.

Small Acts

Small acts, the results of South Slavic female symbology and humanities, facilitate movement that heals our often fragmented, repressed, raw, and wounded physical senses. Through intensified learning applications, our daily life practices and life experiences lead us to perform repetitive movements altered to accommodate our present circumstances. The movements are not necessarily body-oriented; rather, their focus is on shaping a postural attitude that plugs into our senses, affective states, and neurological networks.

The Blood and Honey Icon Storied Aprons small acts section contains examples of what is indicated for postural attitudes. The following questions are found on Blood and Honey Icons Storied Aprons:

Have you searched for your mother's apron? Do you have an apron with wide pockets? Did you ever have curiosity about grandmothers' apron pockets?

How have we women forgotten the unbroken grandmother/mother/daughter lineage?

What recipes, photos, or dolls would you put in the apron pockets to hand down to future generations?

Storied Instructions: An Evolutionary Witness-Bearing Practice to Collectivize Memory

A storied instruction is a term found throughout the Blood and Honey material and encompasses my kolo trauma work in Bosnia since March of 1999. Storied instructions are found in first person stories and the narratives of your life experiences that must be layered over past memories to create new memories in the present. Storied instructions—first person stories—prompt inquiries and profound questions that are not meant to be answered immediately, if ever. Rather, inquires are to be incorporated into daily life practices as part of a well-honed discipline. Storied instructions open the deepened ways of "knowing." All in all, the storied instructions often require years, if not a lifetime, of inquiry, questioning, and practices.

The storied instructions are an archive of trauma-filled narratives of women's wisdom, a learning process so keen that it ripples through their lives, our lives, and those of future generations. Given a sense of place and space, storied instructions are memory that translates trauma into a fruitful learning experience.

We must also note what does not constitute storied instructions. Replacing the intensified learning process of late is a "rubber necking" of sorts, as in the almost obsessive watching of gruesome accidents, creating a "bystander effect." Storied instructions genuinely invite in curiosity, awe, discovery, exploration, and wonder as opposed to voyeurism. The impact of storied instructions is an immediate response: empathy and intensified learning.

Storied instructions invite an empathic understanding of and an intimacy with women's catastrophic memories that commemorate your own healing practice and response. Essentially, your small acts and daily life, full of past memories, are full- bodied storied instructions that link you not just to your local community but to the world at large, both past and present.

References

Paleolithic and Neolithic References for Paleolithic and Neolithic Motifs and Signs

Based on and taken from Gheorghe Lazarovici's *Database for Signs and Symbols of Spiritual Life,* Harald Haarmann, *The Danube Script and Other Ancient Writing Systems: A Typology of Distinctive Features,* Shan M. M. Winn, *The Danube (Old European) Script Ritual use of signs in the Balkan-Danube Region c 5200-3500 BC,* contributors to Institute of Archaeomythology 2008 *Journal of Archaeomythology*[63]

Marija Gimbutas's research, books on Old Europe, 7th millennium BCE

Joan Marler's *From the Realm of the Ancestors, An Anthology in Honor of Marija Gimbutas*

Endnotes

1. Daniel J. Siegel, M.D., *Mindsight: The New Science of Personal Transformation,* Bantam Books Trade Paperback, NY, 2011

2. *Of Human Bonding: Newborns Prefer their Mothers' Voices* Author(s): Anthony J. DeCasper and William P. Fifer Source: Science, New Series, Vol. 208, No. 4448 (Jun. 6, 1980), pp. 1174-1176 Published by: American Association for the Advancement of Science Stable URL: http://www.jstor.org/stable/1683733 Accessed: 28/01/2009 14:55 Study conducted by Anthony DeCasper, University of South Carolina- documented evidence of prenatal learning in the womb by reading of Dr. Seuss and other stories.

3. Daniel J. Siegel, M.D., *The Developing Mind: How Relationships and the Brain Interact to Shape Who We Are,* Guilford Press, NY, p 131-136

4. Julie Mertus, *War's Offensive on Women: The Humanitarian Challenge in Bosnia, Kosovo, and Afghanistan,* Kumarian Press, 2000, p.3.

5. Judith R. Schore, Allan N. Schore, *Modern Attachment Theory: The Central Role of Affect Regulation in Development and Treatment,* Springer Science & business Media, LLC 2007 Clinical Social Work Journal, 2007

6. Eric R. Kandel, *In Search of memory: The Emergence of a New Science of Mind,* W.W. Norton & Company, 2006, "Dramatic achievements of biology during the last fifty years have now made this possible." p.xi

7. Ruth M. Van Dyke, Susan E. Alcock, *Archeologies of Memories,* Blackwell Publishing, 2003, p. 45

8. Steve Pinker, *Stuff of Thoughts,* (Viking, Penguin Group, 2007) p. 141

9. Ken Wilbur, *Spectrum of Consciousness,* Quest Books, 1197, p. 29.

10. *Ibid,* p.29.

11. Yi-Fu Tuan, *Space and Place: The Perspective of Experience.* University of Minnesota Press, 1977, p. 43.

12. *Ibid.,* p. 5

13. Joanna Hubbs, *Mother Russia, The Feminine Myth in Russian Culture,* Indiana University Press, xii-xiii

14. Mona Lisa Schultz, *The New Feminine Brain: How women Can Develop Their Inner Strengths, Genius, and Intuition,* Free Press, 2005 p. 197-202.

15. Judith R. Schore, Allan N. Schore, *Modern Attachment Theory: The Central Role of Affect Regulation in Development and Treatment,* Springer Science & business Media, LLC 2007 Clinical Social Work Journal, 2007

16. http://www.abitabout.com/Oven , Earliest ovens are located in Central Europe, the Ukraine for cooking, roasting and boiling within a structure of a yurt dated at 29,000 BCE. In Ukraine, 20,000 BCE hot coal and ashes were used.

[17] *Ibid*, p. 368

[18] Christopher Knight, Alan Butler, *Civilization One: the World is Not as You Thought it Was.* London,Watkins Publishing, 2004, p. 179.

[19] Milne Holton, Vasa D. Mihailovich, *Songs of the Serbian People,* 1997, p. xii-xiii. "It now seems likely that the day will come when the songs of the South Slavs will be fully recognized by all as a broadly shared cultural heritage, a heritage that may well extend beyond the limits of Slavic Europe.

[20] Christopher Knight, Alan Butler, *Civilization One: the World is Not as You Thought it Was.* London,Watkins Publishing, 2004, p. 179.

[21] Marija Gimbutas, *Civilization of the Goddess,* Harper San Franciso, 1991, p. 56.

[22] Chris Knight, *Blood Relations: Menstruation and the Origins of Culture,* Yale University Press, New Haven and London, 1991, p. 10

[23] Ruth M. Van Dyke, Susan E. Alcock, *Archeologies of Memories,* Blackwell Publishing,2003, p. 45

[24] Peter H. Fraser & Harry Massey, with Joan Parisi Wilcox, *Decoding the Human Body-Field, The new Science of Information as Medicine,* (Healing Arts Press, Rochester, Vermont, 2008) p. 16

[25] Arrien, A., (1987). *The Tarot Handbook: Practical Applications of Ancient Visual Symbols,* Sonoma, CA: Arcus Publishing, p.17.

[26] *Ibid*, p. 17

[27] Bruce Ecker, Laurel Hulley, *Depth Oriented Brief Therapy,* Jossey-Bass Publishers, 1996, p. 109.

[28] West, B., *Epigenetics: Explaining Positive Outcomes* (2011). http://www.seekinghealth.com/blog/epigenetics-definition-positive-outcomes

[29] Sheldrak, Rupert, http://www.sheldrake.org/Articles&Papers/papers/morphic/morphic_intro.html

[30] Ernest L. Rossi, *The Psychobiology of Gene Expression: Neuroscience and Neurogenesis in Hypnosis and the Healing Arts,* W. W. Norton, London, 2002, p. 153

[31] Braden, Gregg, *The Spontaneous Healing of Belief,* Hay House, INC., 2008, p. 13

[32] Joanna Hubbs, *Mother Russia: the Feminine Myth in Russian Culture,* Bloomington: Indiana University Press, 1993, p. 33

[33] Ginot, E., (2007). *Intersubjectivity and Neuroscience: Understanding Enactments and Their Therapeutic Significance within Emerging Paradigms. Psychoanalytic Psychology,* Volume 24, No. 2, 317-332.

[34] Joanna Hubbs, *Mother Russia: the Feminine Myth in Russian Culture,* Bloomington: Indiana University Press, 1993, pp., 61-62.

[35] *Ibid*, p. 61

[36] Rosalind Miles, *Who Cooked the Last Supper? Women's History of the World,* Three Rivers Press, 2001, p. 91

37. Arlene Voski Avakian, Barbara Haber, *From Betty Crocker to Feminist Food Studies: Clinical Perspectives on Women and Food.* University of Massachusetts Press, 2005, p. 9.

38. Marler, J., Dexter M., *Signs of Civilization: Neolithic Symbol System of Southeast Europe,* Published by Institute of Archaeomythology, Sebastopol, CA 95472)

39. Rene Devisch, *Weaving the Threads of Life: the Khita Gyn-Eco-Logical Healing Cult Among the Yaka,* The University of Chicago Press, 1993, p. 134

40. Mona Lisa Schulz, *Awakening Intuition: Using Your Mind-body Network for Insights and Healing,* Three Rivers Press, NY, 1998, p. 81

41. Fortune, Dion, *The Mystical Qabalah,* Weiser Book, Boston, 2000, p.219.

42. Monica Sjoo, Barbara Mor, *The Great Cosmic Mother: Rediscovering the Religion of the Earth,* 1991, p.36

43. Georges Jean, Writing: *The Story of Alphabets and Scripts,* Thames and Hudson, 1994, p. 13

44. Walker, Barbara. *The Women's Encyclopedia of Myths and Secret,* HarperSanFranciso, 1984.

45. Harding, Ester, *Woman's Mysteries, a Psychological Interpretation of the Feminine Principle as portrayed in Myth, Story and Dreams,* Rider & Company, London, 1971, p. 131.

46. Adovasio, J.M., Soffer, Olga, Page, Jake, *The Invisible Sex, Uncovering the True Roles of Women in Prehistory,* HarperCollins, NY, 2007p. 49.

47. *Ibid,* p. 48

48. Marija Gimbutas, *Civilization of the Goddess,* Harper SanFranciso, 1991, p. 400

49. *Ibid,* p. 25

50. Lynne McTagggart, *The Bond, Connecting Through The Space Between Us,* Free Press, NY, 2011, p. 42

51. Marija Gimbutas, *Civilization of the Goddess,* (HarperSanFrancisco, NY, 1991) p. 208

52. Rick Hanson, PH.D., Richard Mendius, MD, *Buddha's Brain, the Practical Neuroscience of Happiness, Love and Wisdom,* New Harbinger Publications, Inc., p. 16.

53. Erich Neumann, *The Great Mother, An Analysis of the Archetype,* Princeton University Press, 1983, p. 39

54. *Ibid,* p. 39.

55. Lloyd DeMause, *Foundations of Psychohistory,* pp. 90-122, 244-332.

56. Monica Sjoo, Barbara Mor, *The Great Cosmic Mother: Rediscovering the Religion of the Earth,* 1991, p.37

57. Marija Gimbutas, *Civilization of the Goddess,* (HarperSanFrancisco, NY, 1991) p. 297

58. Peter H. Frasser, Harry Massey, Joan Parisis Wilcox, *Decoding the Human Body-Field: the New Science of Information as Medicine.* Healing Arts Press, Rocheter, Vermont, 2008, p. 221-231

59. http://scienceworld.wolfram.com/physics/ResonantCavity.html

60. Kenneth Johnson, *Slavic Sorcery: Shamanic Journey of Initiation*, Llewellyn Publications, St. Paul, 1998, p. 64.
61. Rene Devisch, *Weaving the Threads of Life: the Khita Gyn-Eco-Logical Healing Cult Among the Yaka*, The University of Chicago Press, 1993, p. 54
62. Shan M. M. Winn, *The Danube, Old European Script researches the earlier script from southeastern Europe*
63. Institute of Archaeolomythology, Joan Marler, executive director http://www.archaeomythology.org/journal

Endnotes Recipe Section

1. (HarperSanFrancisco, 1991) p.256
2. *Ibid*, p 260- excavated in Radingrad, northeast Bulgaria is a full scale temple (5000 BCE) that had all the working tools of the feminine- dishes, ceramics, oven and loom.
3. Gimbutas, M., *Civilization of the Goddess*, (HarperSanFrancisco, 1991) p. 244
4. http://209.85.173.104/search?q=cache:ahA_vb0Ol60J:hedgerowmobile.com/birch.html+Neolithic+archaeological+besom+broom&hl=en&ct=clnk&cd=14&gl=us
5. Nikola Teslic, *The European Years*, http://www.serbnatlfed.org/Archives/Tesla/tesla-ey.pdf
6. W.R.Ralston p.227-229 Afterwards, the girl dances and spins while the women douse her with water. This practice is thought to convince the heavenly women, clouds, to rain upon the earth, represented by the greenery.
7. John Ayto, *Dictionary of Word Origins*, (Arcade Publishing, New York, 1990) p.332
8. *Ibid*, p. 391
9. Marija Gimbutas, *Civilization of the Goddess* p.22
10. Suzie Jolly & Haxel Reeves, *Gender & Migration*, Institute of Development Studies, University of Sussex, Brighton BN1 9RE, Email: bookshop@ids.ac.uk, Telephone: +44 (0)1273 678269, Fax: +44 (0)1273 621202.
11. The Feminization of International Migration: Issues of Labor, Health, and Family Coping Strategies, http://www.migrationpolicy.org/events/030702_sum.php
12. Brain activity "associated with viewing another person yawn seems to circumvent the essential parts of the MNS [mirror neuron system], in line with the nature of contagious yawns as automatically released behavioural acts–rather than truly imitated motor patterns that would require detailed action understanding," wrote the researchers, with the Helsinki University of Technology and the Research Centre Jülich, Germany. The findings are published in the February issue of the research journal *Neuroimage*."
13. Robert Graves, *ibid.,* 283

Made in the USA
Charleston, SC
20 February 2013